T0121281

It's Time to Play Outside

101 ways for your young child to enjoy independent fun under the sun.

Miska L. Rynsburger

authorHOUSE®

AuthorHouse™
1663 Liberty Drive
Bloomington, IN 47403
www.authorhouse.com
Phone: 1-800-839-8640

First published by AuthorHouse   3/21/2011

ISBN: 978-1-4567-3204-2 (sc)
ISBN: 978-1-4567-5605-5 (e)

Library of Congress Control Number: 2011901059

Printed in the United States of America

Any people depicted in stock imagery provided by Thinkstock are models, and such images are being used for illustrative purposes only. Certain stock imagery © Thinkstock.

This book is printed on acid-free paper.

"I don't want to go outside!"

"There's nothing to do out there."

Ever had either of those gems tossed your way? Odds are, if you are at all involved in the care of young children I just sent shivers up your spine. Hey, of course they don't want to. Why should those kids want to go outside anyway? The house is climate controlled. The closets are stuffed with battery operated toys that do the moving and thinking so the kids don't have to. The TV is inside, not outside. As are the video games. And, unless you're raising your kids in a frat house, there's probably no couch on the front porch for them to loaf around on either. It's OK. Breathe easy. Your kids are normal. It takes more energy and motivation to play outside. Even though it's called playing, your children's bodies are working while outside. It's much easier to stare blankly at the pretty lights in the box in front of you while munching cheese curls than it is to run, jump and play outside with the cold wind on your cheeks. Innately you know it's better for your child to get outside from time to time, but why is it so hard? You know this little person will never again experience a time in life when he will have this much free time to wander through nature, enjoy the sunshine and listen to the birds. It won't be long and he'll be spending at least 7 hours a day sitting in a desk learning followed by 30 years in a cubicle! Now is the time. Today is the day. Get that little person excited about the world outside. It's beautiful and loaded with intriguing discoveries. Outside your child can lay on a carpet that is crawling with living things to watch, feel and listen to…if your child is two years old he might even be tasting some of them. Does your child beg you for a pet? The world outside is teaming with animals waiting to be observed and cared for. Invite your child to lay back and be entertained by the ever-changing ceiling outside.

The purpose of this book is to give you 101 ways to get your child excited to play independently outside. If playing outside is something that has yet to happen in your household, start small. Choose one of the activities you like and think you have what it takes to set it up. If you are excited about the activity, you've just increased the chances that your child will be excited too. I've only included activities that can be set up by you in five minutes or less. Believe me. I know that time is precious. You may have a job, bills to pay, laundry to try to play catch up with, return phone calls to make, not to mention feeding your crowd three meals a day....there I go sending more shivers up your spine. The last thing you have time for in the day is thinking of ways to get your child to want to play outside. This, in fact, is the very reason this book was born. I sent my young children out on a beautiful day to play outside and they came back in several minutes later declaring there's nothing to do out there. With a frozen roast tucked under one arm, a basket of clean laundry to fold in my hands and three bills stuffed in my back pocket I peered out the window and drew a blank. Really? Nothing to do out there, huh? The best I could come up with in the moment was "look again". Weak, I know. I really wanted them to enjoy this beautiful day but my head was so full of how I was going to get everything accomplished today that I just couldn't think of anything for them to do out there either. This book will help you switch from defense to offence. You now have 101 proactive ways to take your children by the hand and in five short minutes set up a creative play activity outdoors. It's important that you come back inside while they play and play and play the day away.

A Word About Independent Play

Independent play is not meant to take the place of time spent with parents. Parents and children spending time together, outside, learning and discussing the changing world before them might just be achieving the trifecta of parenthood. Time and positive attention are among the best gifts a parent can give a child. Nothing should ever take those moments away. On the flip side, the notion that parents should be playing with their children all day is a relatively modern invention. I have a tough time picturing Farmer Brown skipping by the milking cows to play marbles with Jeffery after which they throw the ball around a while and then sketch some still life artwork under the apple tree. Believe it or not, a parent playing with a child all day is not in the best, developmental interest of the child. Independent play teaches a child self-reliance and self-confidence. "If Mom or Dad is always by my side, I'll just go to her or him to solve my problem." When this becomes a life pattern a young child grows up with minimal tools in his tool box to draw from when facing a problem he needs to solve and Mom's not there to bail him out. Playing, exploring and discovering independently is an important way for a child to learn. If Mom blows all the bubbles and explains how they will come out a circle every time, why bother exploring and experimenting anymore? Children need to have alone time to develop their own interests, abilities and skills.

The first generation of children raised by "helicopter parents" are entering the workforce now and it isn't always a pretty sight. Well-intended, loving helicopter parents have been known to barge into their adult child's salary negotiations. Sometimes Mom's wake up call doesn't go through so Johnny's late at the office again. These are not scenarios anyone wants to picture for their grown children. Grown children who lack successful, independent skills were not created over night. These patterns began when the children were small and parents were by their side at every endeavor. It's Time to Play Outside will help parents who want to raise well-rounded, successful children. Set up the outdoor play and let your child play creatively outside, explore, experience, problem solve and create with her own direction, pace, ideas and discoveries.

While pointing this out I'm fully aware that there are four fingers pointing back at me. I know first hand this can be hard. When our first child was born my whole world changed and became complete. I spent every waking minute with that little baby. I blabbered away to her about EVERYTHING, all day! My thought was I didn't bear a child to merely toss the baby aside so I could go about my business of making meatloaf surprise and scrub toilets. My new purpose in life was born when our daughter was born. I had a whole world to show her and discover with her. I've since had to learn and consciously decide to let her learn and discover alone sometimes. Most importantly it's good for her. But I've also found that I can clean the house and still find the time to whip up some dinner for meatloaf Monday. Believe me, I am trying to relinquish my helicopter pilot's license but it's not easy. Though it may be tough, allowing your child to play alone sometimes is in her best interest to help her develop into a confident, independent, healthy person. If your child is playing outside and you need a hug, go find a tree or wait for the mailman to come rolling by. Let your playing child play. Soon enough you can enjoy more time together talking about the fun discoveries she made today.

Why Bother with the Messy Outdoors?

That "on" button is so easy isn't it? Turning on the electronic babysitter provides an "off" button to the noise and busyness in the house. That said, I don't have enough space in this book to detail how important outdoor play is for your young children and you probably don't have the time to get into all the cognitive, emotional, social and physical benefits either. Since you've purchased this book we'll assume you're interested in helping your child spend more time playing outdoors. Good move. I'll take a few moments of your time to show you how and why you are shaping your children's lives in a positive direction.

Most children are born wired with two needs in order to realize their emotional health potential. They need a positive connection with an adult and children need connection to the natural world. Human beings are born well adapt to the outdoor world. In fact, many studies of children in nature conclude that children respond more positively in nature than their adult counterparts because they have not yet had the time to adapt to the artificial, indoor environment. A lack of physical outdoor activity is linked with an ugly plethora of problems. Studies show that children can wind up with obesity and/or obesity related diseases including Type 2 diabetes, high blood pressure, heart disease, asthma, nonalcoholic fatty liver disease, vitamin D deficiency, stress, depression, attention deficit disorder and myopia. Dr. Daphne Miller, a physician affiliated with the University of California, San Francisco, calls them "diseases of indoor living". Adults typically view the world outdoors as a backdrop for their activities whereas, for children, nature is the ultimate stimulator of their activities. It is not simply the scene or landscape in which they are moving. It is, rather, the total sensory experience in which they are engaged. Anything and everything a child needs for play can be found in both nature and by what is inspired in the young child's mind.

Unfortunately, over the past two decades childhood has moved indoors. The Centers for Disease Control found that 6% of children play creatively outside in any given week. *GULP* Those children who are playing outside are often doing it in structured activities under the guidance and direction of an adult, such as a soccer game or fishing derby. If we're hoping our children will get their outdoor time at school that's disappearing as well. Since the No Child Left Behind mandate, 30% of kindergarten classes have no outdoor recess time in their day in order to reach the academic standards set before them.

Let me cut to the chase with some good news. Your young child is wired to play and in fact thrive outside. Here are a few reasons why you should bother to turn the electronic screens off and allow creative outdoor play:

- Outdoor exertion leads to better quality sleep
- Reduced risk of obesity and obesity related diseases
- Stronger bones and lower cancer risk from the Vitamin D obtained by soaking in the sun's rays.
- Studies of school children who play outdoors regularly show these children behave better, are less fidgety and less disruptive
- Increased self-confidence from learning skills such as running, jumping and climbing. This confidence leads to motivation to try new things.
- Understanding and appreciation of the natural world is developed (once you got that, it's tough to shake) and all five senses are expanded.
- Deepened ability to wonder. Wonder is a trademark quality of a lifelong learner. A quick side note: Interviews of potential job candidates at Cal Tech's Jet Propulsion Lab are often asked about their outdoor play experiences as a child because they've found a direct correlation between creative play and superior problem-solving skills.
- Studies show that less time staring at an electronic screen and more time spent stimulated by the natural world decreases the risk of developing near-sightedness.
- Let me throw you back to your chair in human physiology a moment. Beta-endorphins are released in the brain during outdoor play. These are polypeptides which bind to neuro-receptors and are able to work

all kinds of magic in your child's brain. These chemicals are able to relieve pain, enhance the immune system, reduce stress, bring about a sense of well-being and calmness and delay the aging process. Ever think of trying the swing set instead of a new jug of Oil of Olay?

- Longer attention spans that children are naturally born with are not soaked away by hours of Sponge Bob and other TV cronies.
- Imagination and creativity levels remain high through hours of play, thought and wonder outside.

The list really does go on but I'll hop off this soapbox now. The point is, find a way for your child to run, jump, yell, climb, chase, splash in the mud, do all those things that they are not allowed to do inside. Parents set the tone for children. If you start young in the toddler years, your child will develop the habit of outdoor play as an important part of his life and who he is. Don't allow his sense of wonder and imagination to be soaked up by Sponge Bob. Once it's gone, it's tough to get back. All children need to be raised in an environment where they are allowed to thrive cognitively, physically, emotionally, and socially that they may each realize his or her full potential.

How to use this book

Begin by reading through or scanning the activities described. Find a few that catch your eye. The only activities allowed into this book take five minutes or less for you to set up. The creative play ideas are meant for your child to participate in, not you. Spend five minutes in set up and then explain to your child what there IS to do outside today. Rely on your child's imagination and simply let his play begin.

To get creative, outdoor play started never ask your child, "Do you want to play Super Heroes today?" If you give him the choice while he's laying on the warm floor with his feet in the air the answer is likely to be "naw". You set the structure for the day by telling your child in the morning that after his lunch today he'll be playing Super Heroes outside. If he asks you how to play, keep him in suspense by telling him he'll find out after lunch. Follow through by taking him outside at the appointed time and setting him up for Super Hero play. Remember outdoor creative play is an important part of a child's healthy lifestyle. Don't give in to the grumbles before play has even started. Stay strong. You wouldn't let him eat all his Halloween candy in one sitting either right? It's not good for him. You know this and he doesn't. One of the responsibilities of parenthood is to enforce what is best for your child. With good reason, parenthood is also known as wetblankethood. They probably forgot to mention that in the birthing class you took before your baby was born.

Make sure your child has a safe area to play creatively outdoors from which you can easily supervise from. For your child to really develop those independent, self-reliant skills you'll need to let him play alone so he can depend on himself and his imagination to carry the play.

Got a tough nut to crack? Some kids are more natural in the world outdoors than others. If your child throws in the towel after only a few minutes of play it's OK to tell your child that right now is "Outdoor Time". Send him back outside to continue playing. After your child experiences about a dozen of these outdoor creative play activities you'll find that he will get better at playing outside and he'll be comfortable spending more time outside if he knows that coming inside before the play is complete is not an option. Your child's creative mind will expand as will his knowledge base of how to play outside. Like all learned skills, kids get more familiar with how to play creatively the more they experience it.

Try to set aside one regular time every day that your child plays alone outside. If he knows this is a regular part of his day he'll learn to expect it. You can set up his creative play in merely five minutes. Believe me, I know how tempting it is to simply push play and guarantee yourself 90 minutes of quiet to organize your house and mind. Unfortunately those 90 minutes spent staring at the tube are dulling your child's ability to think creatively and to have his own innovative thoughts. You can still have your 90 minutes of quiet and your child can play creatively outside if you follow the activities in this book. Turn off the TV and set up some creative play. Your child's imagination, self-confidence, self-reliance and outdoor skills and knowledge will improve if you give him simply five minutes of set up. It's time to play outside.

SUMMER

Off to the Races!

Materials: sidewalk chalk, several bug volunteers, small container

Ladies and Gentlemen (and Bugs) start your engines! Who doesn't love the thrill of a race? It appears almost instinctual, when two or more children gather together at some point there's bound to be a race. In this activity it's not actually the children racing, it's the bugs. To get the race started you will need to grab some sidewalk chalk and draw several concentric circles on the concrete. The race starting line is actually the smallest, innermost circle in the center. The finish line is the largest, outermost circle. When the lines have been drawn, give your child a little collecting container. Tell your child to go hunting for and gathering up several bugs that look like good athletes ready to show off their mad skillz. Once he has a sufficient number of bugs in his little container your child is ready to prepare his bugs for the races. Your child should carefully place all the bugs in the center circle and declare, "Runners take your mark, get set, GO!" After all the build up, now the job is to sit and watch, wait and observe. No fair budging them along. Likely one bug will start moving, any direction is appreciated and soon the rest will follow. You'll hear your child cheering the racers on, getting louder and louder as one pushes toward the finish line. Soon, your child can declare a winner. Once all the racers have crossed the finish line your child should carefully collect the exhausted little athletes and retire them back to where they were found. Round two can begin with a new group of fresh racers who are raring to go. When the activity concludes be sure to ask your child who he had expected to win and why? What surprised him during the race? The more your child can practice verbalizing the details of his experiences the better. This helps your child's brain recall the order of the event, what his expectations were as well as what he learned and concluded from the activity. These are all great skills for the budding learner.

Summer Stream

Materials: hose, dirt, sticks, stones

Whether it's the happy bubbling sounds or the fact that water is constantly changing form, I have never found a child who is not attracted to a stream. I believe it is one of the laws of nature. You put your children by a stream and within 60 seconds those little explorers will be wandering about in the water; shoes, no shoes, it doesn't matter. It's as if they can't help themselves. Sadly, not all of us are fortunate enough to raise children with a happily, bubbling brook in the backyard. That doesn't have to stop you from allowing your kids to enjoy the exploration of moving water. If you can't bring your children to a stream, why not bring the stream to your children? Simple enough right? Unwind that garden hose on a warm, summer day. Find a spot in the yard that has a slope, keeping in mind the bigger the slope the more fun experimenting your children will have. Crank the hose on and let that water begin cascading down the slope or backyard hill. While the water is saturating the earth, your children can prepare for the fun by each filling a bucket with dirt. Their task will be to help shape the stream by building low walls along the edge of the water path. The real fun begins by creating a dam. Encourage your children to use sticks, stones and mud to help strengthen the force of the dam. Are they able to stop the flow of water? Did they redirect the path of the water with the dam? Or was a waterfall created? What happens when your children change the force of the water from the hose a little slower or a little faster? Float a variety of objects down the stream to see what objects float the farthest or fastest in the water. The possibilities are endless. What a great way to experience the joys of water right in your own backyard.

Ant Restaurant

Materials: scrap of cardboard or tag board, few condiments from the kitchen, paper, pencil

Ants are a marvel to children. Unfortunately, children are a nightmare to ants as soon as those curious, little fingers can start pinching. Young children love to watch these little, black dots bustling busily around on the sidewalk. Alas, these little, black, moving dots are often not quite fast enough to escape the reach of an inquisitive baby. I'm sorry to say our family has had a good many ants that have lost their lives in the name of science at the hands of our little 10-month-old scientists. With a little more direction that young scientist, now with a few more years of life experience and a deeper level of empathy, can carry out a much more humane experiment on these amazing, little creatures. Over a meal, talk with your child about what foods he would expect an ant to prefer to eat and why (I know, you never saw yourself discussing bugs' diets over a meal but, here you are). Have your child choose four foods from the pantry or refrigerator he expects ants might like to eat. Help him put a quarter sized blob on a piece of cardboard or tag board. Now your child must head for the yard in search of a hungry looking group of ants. They can be found in the grass, the sidewalk, a bike path (although be wary of the bike path, bikers can be found there as well), or the driveway. Once a good colony has been identified, set the restaurant within "ant sniffing" distance and have your child observe, no pinching this time please. You may encourage your entomologist to list each food used and tally how many ants chose each delicacy. How did they do with their predictions? Were they surprised?

*hint: in order to help your child achieve a certain level of success in this experiment be sure he chooses something sweet; for example syrup, molasses, sugar granules, etc.

Singing in the Rain

Materials: any and all umbrellas you can find in the house, one lawn chair per child

There's something about the tap, tap, tapping of the rain falling on an umbrella that almost seems magical to young children. Unfortunately, parents are not able control the precipitation outdoors. On a warm, summer afternoon when it seems your child's outdoor creative play could use a little shot in the arm, grab all the umbrellas in the house including the biggest one you have. Can you find any extra large sized umbrellas like a beach umbrella or old, patio umbrella? Set the largest umbrella you could find in the middle of the yard (by now, your children's curiosity is sure to be piqued. Don't let them know what you're up to at this point. Let the suspense build). You may find you want to have the large umbrella standing straight up or simply lay it on its side. Place one lawn chair for each child half in and half out of this large umbrella. Attach any other umbrellas to these chairs with ropes, bungee cords or wiggled between the fabric strips of the chair. Tell your children to take a seat in a chair and then turn on the sprinkler so it hits the umbrellas. That's all it takes. The novelty of something so different, the feel of the water and the sound of the 'raindrops on the umbrellas' will stir the imagination enough for tons of afternoon fun. Head back into the house and watch as your children challenge themselves running in and out of the water trying to dodge the "summer rain drops". At times they might just sit a spell and listen to the sound of the falling rain hitting the umbrellas. Now, about that laundry....

Car/Bike Wash

Materials: dirty car or bikes, sponges, hose, soapy bubbles

Something about dirty cars, hoses and kids that just seem to go together on a hot, summer day. Of course, you ask your husband and he'll probably tell you it is cars, hoses and bikini clad women but that's another book. Rather than taking your car through the car wash, stay at home and enlist the help of your children. Get everyone dressed in old play clothes (that flattened Mayfly on the grill just doesn't look so hot on your daughter's new, summer dress) and fill a bucket with soapy water. Turn on the hose and they can start washing. A word of caution about water with play, if your children are young or nutty, thrill seekers this activity must be supervised closely. A bucket with only two inches of water can pose a danger for young ones. Once the car is suds up, start blasting the hose. I've completed this stage before realizing the moon roof on top of the car had been wide open. You'd think the water cascading inside the car would have tipped me off but apparently not. Learn from my mistake and keep all windows, sun roofs and those sneaky moon roofs closed right from the start. While I can't claim to be an auto detailing expert, I do know that all the soap must be rinsed off the paint of the car. Therefore, it would be wise to intervene at the end of this activity to ensure all the soap has been washed off your squeaky clean car. If one looks closely, one would notice that our car is often cleaned in rainbow streaked patterns from about 4 feet and down. Above that line the dust, squished bugs and bird droppings are often untouched. Our cars will look better as our children get taller. If you don't want the concern of a half washed car have your children wash their bikes. Bikes are always dirty and your child will be able to reach from the top to the bottom for a complete cleaning.

Worm Hotel

Materials: moist soil, dark cloth, a few lucky worms

Has it been raining for forty days and forty nights? Forget the ark. You're probably all about ready to hop aboard the crazy train! What you may not know is that, under these conditions, your yard is teeming with hundreds of worms crawling up from out of the dirt in search of air to breathe and buddies to save them. We're quickly going from bad to worse aren't we? Before you're completely disgusted and turn the page, allow me a few more minutes. If there is a small break in the rain clouds you can send your children out on an important rescue mission. Cover them up with rubber boats, rain coats, whatever the weather requires and let them know someone needs to save those poor worms in the yard. The worms have come crawling out of the dirt because the rain water has flooded their tunnels and homes. Consequently, they can't breathe. They come squiggling out of their dark world and enter the world above in search of fresh air. Unbeknownst to them when the rain clouds dissipate and the sun begins to shine again these little guys will be sitting ducks if they happen to be on any form of cement at the time. They will fry faster than your Aunt Margie can whip up some scrambled eggs, might not look much better either. Your child can fill a glass bowl or large, glass jar with loose soil. When the jar is full he should stir the dirt with a stick to ensure there's plenty of fresh air for the incoming occupants. Now the new residence is ready for those insane worms who thought they could take on the concrete. Don't let your child go overboard. He should choose a humane amount of worms to save. Your child can carefully set the worms on top of the dirt and watch as they acclimate themselves to their new home. Soon your child will probably naturally seek out a few sticks and leaves to add, creating some nice ambiance for the worms. If you decide to allow your child to 'overnight' with the worms be sure to cover the jar with a dark cloth to allow the moisture to stay in the hotel. Nobody likes a cooked pet, even if it is a worm.

Good Ole' Daisy Chain

Materials: Daisies or Dandelions, fairy dust (bag of glitter or sugar)

This activity is a favorite, time honored outdoor pass time and can be used to help a child transform her world into a land of flowers and fairies. It does require nimble fingers, however. In order for this activity to be completed independently your child will need to be very comfortable and confident with tying a knot. If that skill is not in place I'm afraid you'll find your child in a frustrated, befuddled mess of stems, stains and tears. Your child can prepare for the fun by picking a large bouquet of daisies or dandelions (a great way to rid the yard of some stubborn weeds for a day or two). Keep the stems as long as possible. Demonstrate for your child how to tie the bottom of one flower stem to the top of another stem, just below the flower head. When the knot is complete your child has the first chain link. She can continue tying one flower stem to the previous flower just below the head. When she feels the flower chain is long enough for a headband, wristband, necklace or sash your child can tie the last two flower end pieces together. Before setting her new tiara and bracelet in place your child may want to get dressed up in her "fairy clothes" to help get the imagination and creative thinking rolling. With her new adornments your flower fairy will be ready to begin spreading magic throughout the yard. One more long stemmed flower can serve as her magic wand. Give your dressed up fairy a little bit of magic, fairy dust a.k.a. bag-o-glitter. If glitter is not handy at the moment a little bit of sugar in a baggie will also work. While it's not ideal for your child to have easy access to sugar, ingesting too much salt can actually be dangerous. If you see your fairy licking her fairy dust rather than sprinkling throughout the kingdom you may be better off to forego the magic fairy dust this time. Encourage your fairy to attach any dandelion or clover flower she can find to trees braches, bushes and tree bark. She can fly around the yard bringing about summertime to the land.

Mud Pies

Materials: aluminum pie plates or paper plate bowls, spoons, pitcher of water, measuring cup

Just finished dinner? Now you're hoping to clear the table, load the dishwasher, get a little laundry done and straighten the house aren't you? Setting the bar pretty high. On those days when it really matters, it might be time to pull out the big guns. Tell your children dessert is their responsibility tonight. Get them set up in their "kitchen", or area of the yard with some dirt that could stand a little extra moisture. They'll need a pitcher of water and some aluminum pie plates. If you don't have a fresh supply of disposable pie plates hanging around the cupboards, paper plate bowls or disposable plasticware works pretty well too. Each child will also need a spoon and if you can part with it, the measuring cup which will allow them to practice with concepts like volume and liquid measurements. Tell your children their task will be to bake up a whole fresh supply of mud pies for all to enjoy. What could be better for dessert? As your chefs are whipping up their concoctions you'll find you've got time to fly through your tasks. Children love being involved in the cooking process to any given degree. You'll see them adding a yummy smattering of goodies to the recipe that began with merely water and dirt. There they are happily creating, stirring, sharing and playing. Before you know it the house is in great shape, you've had a chance to read the article in the paper you could only glance at this morning and you've even returned a few calls. The best part, for those muddy little folks outside? By the time you call them in it's bath time.

Shmuk Tag

Materials: large sponge, several buckets of water

Tag is a time honored game that is a delightful mix of racing and catching your opponent. A form of tag is really one of the first games babies enjoy playing. Ever see adults hide behind their hands and ask, "Where did Momma go?" "Peek-a-boo!" Yup. Baby form of tag. Shmuk tag is a version of tag that is best played outside in the summertime on a hot day. Grab a few buckets from the sand box and fill them up with water. Set the buckets throughout the yard in locations that mark the boundaries of play. The person who is "it" is given the biggest sponge you are able to find, like car washing kind. The objective for the sponge bearer is to get that sponge soaking wet and throw it on one of the runners. Faces are off limits. If one of the runners gets shmuked he becomes "it". In this version of tag there's no disagreements about whether or not a runner's been hit. If you've got a wet spot, you've been shmuked.

*variation: if you've got children of different ages and varying abilities, some might be a little young for the speed and agility needed to play tag. They might enjoy playing toss with the big, wet sponge instead. Place a bucket at the feet of each participant. Each bucket should be filled with water at a comfortable temperature. Set your young players close together as that big, wet sponge can be quite a heavy load. Saturate the sponge, hand it off to an eager child and let the tossing begin. Your children will find this activity a fun way to practice eye hand coordination all the while staying cool on a hot afternoon. A word of caution with water play and young children; anytime you add water in your children's play, close supervision is necessary. Accidents happen easily and quickly.

Cozy as a Bug in a Jar

Materials: old jar, grass clippings, leaves

No matter where you are found, bugs follow summertime and children follow bugs. If you can't beat that truth you might as well make the best of it. Children love caring for animals great or small. I know this. I've lived it. I once fell in love with a beetle and named him Blackie. Poor Blackie. I don't remember exactly what it was that brought about his demise but I'm afraid it might have something to do with being held captive in a jar in a little girl's room too long. I'm sure the air circulation in that jar wasn't the finest. Likewise, my daughter fell in love with a slug. She took great care of that little, ugly creature. It wasn't an easy task convincing my daughter to let her go. I was, by the way, informed in no uncertain terms the slug was a girl. You could tell from the slug's eyelashes. My mom, I'm told, used to line spiders up and play school with her unruly students. Talk about a teacher nightmare. I'll save all of this for another book one day on mental health or the lack thereof as the case may be. You likely have a few bug or small critter stories of your own from your past. Allow your child to befriend a bug. There are plenty of bugs who won't bite and can be quite tolerable to the open mind. Give your child an old, washed out jar and tell him to fill it with a layer of dirt on the bottom, some leaves and sticks for shelter and exercise. It won't take your child long to spot a victim, I mean, pet in the yard. Keep that little fella in the jar for a short time. Let your child feed it, take it for a walk, talk to it a bit and show it the yard. However, it too has a family it must really be getting back to so soon it must be released back to its home. In the meantime, your child will feel good about the afternoon adventure he provided a little somebody.

AUTUMN

Leaf Centerpiece

Materials: one vase per child, bendable straws, colorful leaves, sticks with berries

Deciduous leaves, those are the kinds that fall off the trees, are beautiful in the fall. Maples provide the striking reds and yellows. Oaks add to the display with yellows and browns. The autumn leaves differ from tree to tree. As the temperature cools, the trees begin to shut down and no longer need food from the green leaves. The water supply to the leaves stops which in turn shuts down the green chlorophyll. As the chlorophyll disappears the brilliant fall colors begin to showcase themselves. This might be helpful information in case your little botanist asks you why the leaves change colors in the fall or if you ever find yourself in a stint on Jeopardy. Have your child get out in the yard experiencing these fall beauties. Present your child with a bud vase stuffed with straws and you'll have her attention and interest. A straw filled vase is something she's never seen on a TV commercial, never saw her friend carrying around and never read about in a book. This is a vase now begging to have each of its little cubbies filled with something. Send your child out into the yard, vase in hand, ready to fill each little hole with something unique and beautiful. She'll have fun watching her bouquet come to life. Once all the straws are filled she can now complete the arrangement by bending the straws creating exactly the right look. Be careful not to get over zealous and send her out with the huge crystal vase you bought on your honeymoon. Risk #1: your child might lose interest before filling the 113th straw. Risk #2: the next time you see this vase it might be shattered into 918 pieces all over the driveway. A bud vase with about 15 straws is a nice way to begin this project. When the bouquet is brought back to you be sure to declare how beautiful it is no matter what you're looking at. Clear a corner somewhere in the house and exclaim what beauty is now added to this once drab corner. This positive reinforcement will teach her that her work and ideas are valued.

Buried Treasure

Materials: healthy snacks in a bag, leaf pile or sandbox

Do your kids fancy themselves puppies from time to time? Robots? Aliens? Children are blessed with amazing imaginations that can transport them to other places and times. An imagination that has not yet been dulled by DVD's and video games is able to change a child into any being imaginable. Our children like to fancy themselves rabbits from time to time. Now I have no idea what Freud and his cronies would say about rabbits personified but I like to take advantage of it. On a beautiful fall day rake a good amount of leaves to one side of the lawn and encourage your children to morph into their favorite animals or toys. When there are enough leaves to play in, fill a good amount of plastic snack bags with one healthy snack. One snack item per bag (you're going to make them work for today's snack). I usually use carrot sticks for our rabbits. Send your children scurrying to the other side of the yard and quickly bury those bags with snacks in the leaf pile. If you don't have enough leaves in the yard to build a pile, the sandbox will work just as well. A few moments later call your children to come scampering back to begin their digging and searching. Once all the bags have been recovered they can repeat the play with each other. If you have only one child playing he can throw them in the air, stir the leaves with his eyes closed and begin the search again. When hunger overtakes your children, they will enjoy a snack in the sunshine. Remember, when the play begins be sure to exit. Allow them to persevere in the search independently, working together to recover the snacks. If you stick around, they'll invariably ask for hints and help to get their snacks. Besides, you probably need to wash all the fingerprints off the windows. They always look exceptionally bad on those beautiful, sunny days.

Leaf Letter

Materials: ten most beautiful leaves from the yard, friend from a different climate's address, envelope

Outdoor time can be a chance for your child to experience unstructured playtime when he can think and act creatively. However, there will be times your child's play may need a little boost to get the creativity rolling. In this activity you can offer your child a mission to complete. Discuss with your child about a friend or family member who lives in a different climate. Talk about how climate affects your lives differently than the affects experienced by your friend or family member. Certain leaves are unique to specific climates found throughout our country. With your child's help address an envelope to the friend or family member you've been talking about. Take a quick peek on the family computer, map or globe showing where your home is compared to this friend's home. Talk about the distance from the equator and how heat dissipates the further north you are. Even if your child is very young it's great for them to be exposed to this language and these ideas, though at times it may look like you're talking to a butterfly. With this understanding and the addressed envelope, send your child outside in search of the best leaves he can find. He should tuck all his favorite leaves into the envelope. Once the envelope is full of the best leaves he can find, your child can take out each of the leaves and lay them on the driveway or other cleared area to pick out the top ten most beautiful samples of leaves from your area. Once the top ten have been chosen your child has a unique gift to send to a friend or family member.

*note: if you don't have a friend or family member somewhere else in the country I'm sure Jack Nicholson in Las Angeles, CA or Martha Stewart in Maine wouldn't mind a few envelopes filled with leaves ☺

Pumpkin People

Materials: old pants, old zip up coat, string, leaves or yard clippings

We've all done it. Admit it. There's a pair of jeans in your child's drawer you are hanging on to trying to squeeze one more season out of. It's not pretty. You know it. You've put your son in these jeans to play in and he's running around the yard donning a pair of cute Capri's. Good news. You've now got a much more respectable use for those old pants. Your child can get one last hurrah with the jeans making a pumpkin person. Tie off the bottom of each pant leg with some string, craft yarn or a couple of rubber bands. Essentially, your child now has two empty bags waiting to be filled one last time before the jeans make their trip to Goodwill, the neighbor kid or wherever yesterday's goodies end up. For the upper body, tie off the two sleeves of an old shirt or coat at the wrist and bunch the waist together tying tightly. Armed with these old duds, send your child out to the yard charged with bringing life to his pumpkin person. Each garment must be over stuffed with leaves. The more tightly crammed in the better. Remember this rule of thumb when making pumpkin people: Slim Sam turns into a Sad Sack after about a day. Once the clothes are jammed with leaves carefully place a pumpkin head in its place. You may find it best to assist in this task or heads may roll, literally. Don't be surprised if you witness the Florence Nightingale effect. Your child may become so attached to the pumpkin person he brought to life you may find he wants to play outside near his new friend all day. Keep your eyes on the weather with your pumpkin people outside. If you see rain in the forecast, that's a good time to take the folks apart. It doesn't take much fall rain to turn a dapper looking pumpkin gentleman into Quasimodo slumping on your front steps. The "hand-me-down" potential for the clothes will be out the window if they sit in wet leaves for any length of time.

House of Leaves

Materials: rake, yard full of leaves

Children love playing house. It doesn't take much to awaken the domestic side in even the most energetic of kids. Let the fall leaves fall for a few days without raking (twist, twist). When the yard is covered with leaves you have what you need to create a play house out of leaves. Rake out a pathway to the front door of the house. Help your children see where the outer walls or boundaries of the house are. They can hone their interior design skills by helping to determine where the kitchen should be, bedrooms, bathroom and living room. Clear out rectangles of grass for each room. Your children can use leaves from the yard outside of their house to create tables, tubs, teapots and toilets. They will have fun bringing the house to life using their imagination and leaves. Once everything is in place it's time for the next phase of fun to begin. Your children can play house in their house. Give them a Tupperware container with an afternoon snack to be stowed away in the refrigerator. Set the table with a couple of glasses of water. They can "take a nap" in their bed of leaves. Your children might like to bring out a favorite doll they can care for. Invariably, dolls always seem to need a nap when taken out for play. The doll can be placed in the bedroom and soon after fed a meal in the kitchen. You'll watch your children walking from room to room in their new house chattering away. Best part? No vacuuming, sweeping, laundry to put away or chores to be done. Just creative play.

Speedway

Materials: rake, yard full of leaves

By the time we replace the carpet in our living room there's sure to be a very clear oval grooved into the carpet fibers. This is due to the "running phase" each of our children have lived through. In the evening when baths are completed, pajamas are donned and we are trying to slow the pace of the day something happens to these little bodies. I don't know if they're burning off excess steam from the day or if it's their rebel way of showing it's not actually time for bed. Whatever the cause, our children can be seen involuntarily sprinting laps around the living room floor as fast as their feet will carry them. Sound familiar at all? I have to hope we're not the only household with the late night Carl and Carol Lewis sprinting circles around the coffee table. In the interest of both offering your carpet a few weeks more of life and in getting those energy balls to burn rubber outside rather than inside, rake up two large ovals in the yard full of fall leaves. One oval should fit inside the other creating a racetrack of sorts. Ask your children to go find their "super fast racing shoes" for wearing on the track. No ordinary shoes should ever be worn on this race track. Show your racers where the speedway is, get them to the starting line, call out "On your mark, get set, GO!" and back away. It won't take much for their imagination to take over and the day of racing to commence. The sound of your children's groveling engine voices will be heard soaring throughout the neighborhood as they tear around their track. You may even attract a few guest racers with all the commotion.

*variation: if you don't get a yard full of leaves you can let the grass grow a touch longer than normal and mow a large oval in the yard for the speedway. Dual benefit. Your children will spend the day spinning and racing their wheels AND your husband will probably ask that you never again mow the lawn.

Buried Skeletons

Materials: plant skeletons from the yard, sand box

Did you know that when the temperatures cool in the fall and the leaves are busy falling off the trees those beautiful field flowers are shriveling up and turning into plant skeletons? This is actually a term used by botanists. How about that? Even nature dresses up for Halloween. Meadows and open fields are crawling with skeletons in the fall. Take a walk in an open field with your child to examine some of these weeds turned skeleton. They are the dried out remains of familiar flowers like goldenrod, queen Anne's Lace, tansy, mugwort, among others. Snap the neck of a few samples (yeah, getting carried away with word choice) and bring them home. Let your child have a little fun with these fall wonders before really dissecting them. Bury those old bag of bones in a sandbox. Have your child close her eyes and begin feeling around in the sandbox for anything long, hard and crusty. Encourage your child to keep her eyes closed and "see" the old weed with her fingers. How does it feel different than it might have in the spring? Once all the skeletons have been recovered from the sand she can lay them all in a clean, well lit area. Carefully shake the sand free and begin to examine each skeleton one at a time. Working like a CSI team member can your child identify or recognize what each skeleton used to look like in its hay day? Believe it or not, some of these old skeletons still have some smell leftover. Your child can crush some of the shriveled, harden flowers and smell. Does that give you a hint as to what this flower used to be? Bear in mind, many of these skeletons have some amount of fluff on them somewhere which is the propellant for the seeds ready to take flight. Be careful that a young one doesn't wind up with nostrils full of goldenrod fluff. She'll be sneezing the rest of the night. While cleaning up, talk together about what your child may have learned or discovered. Just remember this: Why are skeletons so calm? Because nothing gets under their skin! Ba doom, ting!

WINTER

Winter Blocks

Materials: muffin tins, paper cups, Tubberware containers, ice cube tray

Children innately love stacking things. The only thing that might be more gratifying for the young child busy stacking a pile of blocks is knocking them down and watching the whole tower go crashing to the floor. That is, unless older brother was the one who crashed the tower to the floor. Then it's not so fun anymore. Solve that problem on an especially drab, winter day by surprising all your children with a new set of winter blocks for each of them. Before going to bed the night before simply fill up some muffin tins, paper cups, mugs and ice cube trays with water. Do you have any five gallon buckets hanging out in the garage? They make spectacular blocks but also require a bit more freezing time if you don't live in the tundra of Canada. Set the dishes outside to do the work for you over night. By the time your children are up the next morning and ready to play, a new set of blocks will be waiting to be popped out of their containers and played with. To easily pop the winter blocks out of their holder simply take the dishes inside for the length of time it takes to bundle your children up in their winter gear (in my world we're talking about 38 minutes because invariably someone always has to go potty again after the last zipper has been zipped and we're all standing there sweating buckets!). The warmth of the house will melt the outermost edges of each block allowing it to be easily slipped right out of its container by simply turning it upside down. No chiseling or prying required. Give each child her own set of blocks and send them outside to build and create with their new blocks. These blocks can be used to construct a beautiful ice palace, a warm igloo for plastic figurines to ward off the winter winds, or a tall tower waiting to be smashed to the ground. When play is done for the day this time Mother will pick up after you. Mother Nature that is. Now if we could just talk her into unloading the dishwasher from time to time as well.

Snow Buddy

Materials: snow, sticks, stones

Snowmen can be so much fun to make but they are often more the effort of the adults as opposed to a creation of the children. I have yet to see a three foot tall child heaving a four foot snowball around the yard. Building a snowman is a great family bonding experience. However, once the snowman has been created the task is pretty well complete. There's not much more you can do with the big, white guy except look at him. We've tried crafting a snowman on a sled so he could be transported throughout the yard but he ended up in desperate need of a body transplant. Too many tears involved to ever try that idea again. A fun, tear-free fix to the stationary snowman is making a snow buddy. These little guys are very portable, mendable and lovable. Your child begins by shaping a snowball. If her hands are not quite nimble enough for this task inside her mittens or if her fingers can't quite meet in the middle because her coat is so thick (think Ralphie's little brother in <u>A Christmas Story</u>) you may need to shape about a dozen solid snowballs for her. Your child now brings life and personality to each of these little creatures. Using pine needles for hair, sticks for arms and legs, pebbles for eyes and a smile she's got herself a small, portable snow buddy to care for. Don't be surprised if your child begins to create friends for her buddy as well as a few parents. She'll probably craft some sort of shelter for these little buddies. When purchasing a cuddly toy from the store inevitably your child is going to see the back of the packaging and begin to want the car, ramp, store, house and rest of the toys that go with this set. Those toy companies know what they're doing! Without spending a cent your child can now create the complete set for her snow buddy! All the friends can be made, houses, stores, ramps and tunnels to crawl through. Soon your yard will transform into a bustling town for snow buddies! Why buy it when your child can build it?

Restaurant

Materials: paper plates, plastic tableware

Ever thought it might be a nice idea to treat yourself to a night out at a restaurant with the family? I once had an innocent thought like that as well. It's probably been a busy week for you and a break from cooking would hit the spot. Upon arriving at the establishment and being ushered to your table your two year old trips over his untied shoe laces which sends him flying into an unsuspecting waiter toppling the tray of beautifully arranged desserts. You pull your child out of the mess of whipped cream and chocolate syrup while he takes a quick swipe at the goodies from the floor and sucks on his finger. When the destroyed desserts are cleaned and all apologies are behind you, you then continue on to be seated at your table. While peering over the menu trying to decide what the children will actually eat and not pick at your one year old in the high chair begins chucking crayons at the couple behind you. After plucking the violet-red, all the while smiling apologetically, from the nice lady's hair you settle on your dinner choices. While trying to place your order with the waitress your two year old and four year old are arguing about whose glass is whose and which fork belongs to whom. By the time food has been chosen for the entire group these two have taken matters into their own hands and are now dueling, each armed with a butter knife. Your husband reaches to take the knives away and his elbow knocks over your one year old's glass of water. Why did your one year old have a glass of water anyway!?! The ice cold water makes its way across the table and, as if in slow motion, it cascades on to your two year old's lap. He, of course, screams. Well, the plus side, the duel is now over but you've got a two year old in a pair of icy, cold, wet pants. Check the diaper bag. There's a pair of pink pants with purple daisies for your 13 month old daughter you may be able to squeeze him into. While getting the pants out of the bag you see the baby in the high chair has assumed the position, going red in the face and has decided this would be a good time and place to dirty her diaper. With the table full of sopping wet napkins, water glasses shoved out of reach and butter knives hidden, your waitress comes to the table with five steaming hot plates of food.

I've been told one day I'll look back on days like this and laugh. Yes. I suppose it wouldn't surprise me either if the sound of my laughter is one day heard echoing down the stark hallways of the loony bin. Until that time, I like to think I know when I've been defeated. How about a nice restaurant experience at home instead for now? If you live in a region with good sized drifts of snow help your children mold a table and stools in their restaurant. Give them some paper plates and plastic tableware, hopefully not all white or you might not see them again until next spring. Your children can become patrons, wait staff, chefs and hostesses. You'll find them role playing, creating and pretending. They can create and eat all their own food. One word of advice if you peek out the window and see a patron gnawing at the corner of the table, remind them to stay away from the yellow snow, and that may be a cue to bring out some real food for a little healthy afternoon snack time.

Winter Olympics

Materials: yard full of snow

Once every four years the world comes together in front of their collective television screens to watch as the excitement, drama and thrill of the Winter Olympics unfolds in living rooms worldwide. You can make your own Winter Olympics excitement, drama and thrill in your yard once a week if your children so desire. Rather than a contest with winners and losers, these Winter Olympics can be thought of as more of an obstacle course surrounding your house. Each participant moves from station to station completing all the winter games. Look at the features of your yard to help you best determine the events for your children. If you have a hill or slope to any degree you'll certainly want to include the sledding event. Some other possibilities are the snowball throw. In this event athletes have to stand behind a line drawn in the snow and throw snowballs until they hit a target like a tree or wall of some sort, hopefully window free. Another stop can be the snow angel station. Each athlete throws themselves into the snow, flings his arms and legs around a bit and makes an angel. The next event can be a "shovel a letter or design in the driveway". Athletes pick up a shovel and dig out the letter they have been practicing or a fancy design in the driveway (let's hope athletes spend a lot of time on this one). The next challenge could be crawling under the swing set slide, the deck or other low structure you can find in your yard. Look around and find a variety of challenges circling around your house. Children will play their way around the yard working through all the stations. When they complete the course they can award their efforts with a gold medal, made of white gold of course. Warm those hard working athletes up with a steaming cup of hot chocolate at the closing ceremonies.

Snow Princess/Soldier

Materials: shovel

If you live in a region with a snowy season and you have small children you've no doubt made the quintessential snowmen and igloos. I don't mean to knock these snowy structures because this kind of creating and playing is fantastic. I just can't include it in this book because everyone already knows about these. How about a new twist on an old favorite? Instead of an igloo try having your child build an ice castle. Dress up your child as a snow princess by applying a little extra chap stick on her lips and Vaseline on her cheeks with a few glitter sprinkles before sending her outside. Give her a baggie of glitter to sprinkle on her royal subjects. Otherwise if your child is more of the soldier type than princess put a hard hat over his ear muffs to toughen him up and arm him with a stick. Now your snow princess or soldier needs a castle to either swoon in or to guard respectively. Help your child get the creative process started (don't tell her highness, but this princess is going to have to build her own digs!). If you have an area near a shoveled walkway or snow blown driveway with several feet of piled snow you've got the ground work for fantastic castle play. Use a shovel to build the stairway up. Dig out a flattened "living area" about two feet in from the top of the snow heap. Your princess or soldier will take over the construction process from this point. He or she can begin placing palace blocks along the top of the living quarters. Broken icicles pointing upward add a nice aesthetic touch but can be a real danger too. Perhaps you might choose to use the icicles as the bars on the dungeon window in which the dragon sits awaiting his fate. Odds are good the castle staff will end up freeing this dragon shortly by eating the bars away. Your child should also fashion a castle gate as well as the roadway out to the rest of the kingdom. Now, you, one of the lowly commoners of the kingdom, better get yourself inside and start grinding the wheat. Your princess or soldier will need to eat more than prison bars and palace blocks today.

Snowflake Investigation

Materials: magnifying glass, black paper or fabric, white crayon, hard surface to write on

Snowflakes are a marvel of nature. If you get snowflakes in your region you are probably familiar with the different types of snowflakes that can be found. There's slush that falls from the sky, pellet balls, sleet, hail, even sideways falling snow. You also know that every once in a great while you get a day with snowflakes that hold their shape all the way from the clouds to the ground. They are the most beautiful crystals falling from the sky. To a child it can seem magical. If they land on a cold surface you can behold their beauty even if for just a moment. You can see that almost all snowflakes have six points. They are white and twinkle in the light. It's one of these moments that should not be lost on your child. Grab the aforementioned materials and rush outside. This moment is worth letting your grilled cheese burn to a crisp. Allow the snowflakes to fall on the darkly colored paper and let your child use the magnifying glass to marvel at each stunning snowflake. If the snowflake holds its shape for long enough ask your child to draw the design she sees with the white crayon on the dark paper. If the snowflake melts away too quickly to copy the design wait a few moments to let the temperature of the paper fall below freezing. In the meantime, your child is likely to open her mouth and catch a little snack falling from the clouds.

*Here's a few fun facts about snowflakes in case your investigator is interested:

Every snowflake has its own unique shape and is different than all other snowflakes.

All snowflakes have six sides.

Snowflakes aren't always white. Years ago, when coal was used in factories and homes, snow was often gray. Why? Because the coal dust entered the air and was absorbed by the clouds.

In Prince Edward Island, Canada, where the soil is red clay, snowflakes often look pink. Why? Because red dust from the soil is blown into the air and absorbed by the clouds.

The largest snowflakes ever recorded fell in the state of Montana in the United States of America. The snowflakes were 15 inches in diameter.

The snow capital of the United States is Stampede Pass in Washington State. Each year, the average snowfall is 430 inches.

The average snowflake falls at a speed of 3.1 miles per hour. (5 kilometers)

Snirt is dirty snow that flies off the dusty Canadian prairies.

People buy more cakes, cookies and candies than any other food when a blizzard is in the forecast.

A blizzard occurs when you can't see for ¼ mile. The winds are always 35 miles an hour or more. The storm must last at least 3 hours to be classed as a blizzard. If any of these conditions are less, it is only a snowstorm.

Billions of snowflakes fall during one short snowstorm.

Snowflakes are made up of ice crystals.

*http://www.suite101.com/article.cfm/science_for_kids/111983

'Tis the Season

Materials: milk jug belt, popcorn, cranberries or grapes,

Before you can get the word "Christmas" to cross your lips, you've already gotten 99% of all kids' attention. Children love to be involved in every aspect of Christmas. Nature offers a treasure trove of beautiful things that can be utilized to decorate a tree or bush in your yard. Ask your child to decorate a chosen tree or bush in your yard that the birds and squirrels might enjoy this holiday season. To ease the task of collecting goodies for the tree make the milk jug belt for your child. You'll find it's a great way for children to collect all sorts of things and keep their two hands free to work. Wash out one milk jug per child. Working at a slant, cut one third of the top of the jug off leaving the handle intact. Now thread a belt through the handle and wrap the belt and jug around each child's waist. Presto! Your child has a wonderful spot to store all her collectables. Sprinkle some pop corn on the bottom of the milk jug for your child to start the decorating. If the chosen tree is a pine tree your child can dust the popcorn on its branches. If the tree or bush is deciduous and has dropped its leaves already your child can poke the kernels on the branch tips. When the pop corn has been placed your child can begin to search the yard over for some fall beauties that often go under appreciated. As an example, our outdoor tree was adorn with dried hydrangeas, a crow's feather, vines from the woods, silver dollars (phlox flowers), long grasses were draped like tinsel, there was even a mushroom poked onto one of the branches. The goal here is to get your child to view this activity not as a one dimensional task to be completed but rather a new way of seeing things throughout the yard. It takes a deeper kind of thinking for your child to evaluate which items might work best as a decoration, express opinions and make decisions about where these newly discovered decorations might go and creatively design an outdoor Christmas tree. While your neighbors might think you've got some strange scientific grafting project going with your tree, you know that your child has spent an afternoon breathing in fresh air, developing her imagination and creativity all the while happily playing and thinking at a deep level.

Snow Painting

Materials: squirt bottle, spray bottle or both, food coloring or Kool-aid packets

For those who live in a snowy region, by the time you're into February you've already probably constructed an army of snowmen and enough snow forts to house said army. By this point in the winter, it is probably time for something new. Wash out a few squeeze bottles and/or spray bottles you might find in the back of your bathroom cabinets. Fill each with water and sprinkle in a little Kool-aid powder for coloring or drop in a bit of food coloring (which I found to be tougher to wash out of mittens and coat sleeves but more vivid results in the snow than the Kool-aid was able to produce). Bundle your children up and let them decorate anything and everything outside with their new coloring tools. The squirt bottles can be used for more detailed designs such as letters and numbers in the snow or for buttons on the snow people dotting the yard. The sky is the limit. The spray bottles are good for the general coloring of a larger area of snow such as blue jeans and a green Mohawk on your snow people (every yard needs a punk snow dude, right?) Let your children get creative and innovative with the colors. Just be sure you wash out the bottles well before placing them in the bathroom cabinet again. It's one thing to have your yard adorn with green haired snow people, it's a whole different issue to have a green haired Mom trouncing around town with her kids.

Who Dunnit?

Materials: freshly fallen snow, stuffed animal holding a bagged snack, binoculars and a magnifying glass

Freshly fallen snow can be so beautiful. On a day when everything looks crisp, clean and white with a new blanket of snow covering the yard you've got the perfect set up for a mystery to involve your children. Grab a stuffed animal that can handle being outside in the snow. Pack a pair of children's binoculars, a healthy snack and a magnifying glass in a brown paper bag and slip into a pair of boots. With the packed bag and the stuffed animal tucked under your arm head outside to create the trail. Walk all over the yard, sometimes zig zagging, sometimes loopty looping, sometimes climbing over things, sometimes crawling under things. The point is to get your little detectives deciphering which direction the culprit's prints are heading and stay hot on the trail. If your neighbor sees you crawling under your deck just shrug and say you lost your contact (he'll probably already assume the long winter has gotten the best of you and you've lost your marbles). When you get to the far reaches of your yard set the stuffed animal perpetrator clutching the bagged goodies and back track to the house following the same trail. Now, help your children bundle up into their warm gear and tell them that their snack was stolen! If they can solve the mystery the snack is theirs! Off they go following the footsteps of the culprit. After a while they should be able to locate and enjoy the stolen goodies. A double reward! The magnifying glass and binoculars are included in the bag to help facilitate further winter investigations now that your children have crime solving on the mind.

Posable Snowman

Materials: old clothes, craft yarn

Who says that snowmen have to be big, fat and round? I don't know about you but it seems to me our buddy Frosty could have benefitted from a visit with Richard Simmons. How about a svelt snowman for a healthy statement in your front yard this season? Most young children are not able to maneuver large enough snowballs around the yard to build the classic snowman independently. The posable snowman, however, is one that a young child can create without much interference from you. Help your child choose a long sleeve shirt he can live without for a day or two and long pants to dress his snowman in. Tie the bottom of each pant leg closed using craft yarn or a rubber band. Close of the waist and sleeves of the shirt with yarn or a rubber band as well. Bring the clothes outside with the instructions for your child to stuff the pants full of snow. When the pants are loaded your child will be able to get the snowman's legs to stand in their spot alone. Next, your child can pack the shirt with snow in the same fashion. When the shirt is as full as possible it can be placed on top of the pants. Now, the snowman can be carefully moved into a variety of poses...remember Gumby? Your child can then pack together a ball of snow and stick in it place for a head. Don't forget the carrot for a nose, pebbles for eyes and a nice toasty hat. So much for the snowman with an obesity problem. This fella's got a cholesterol level that might just make you blush.

Snowy Pet Shop

Materials: stuffed animal buddies or plastic figurines, snow

Playing in a yard full of fluffy white snow is just as fun as the world's biggest sandbox except sand doesn't wash down the throat as nicely. Before jumping into all the winter gear tell your children to gather up a few stuffed animals that can handle the great outdoors or some durable plastic durable plastic animals you may have. These will soon serve as the pets for sale in the new pet shop in town. Help initiate the snowy pet shop creative playtime by shoveling a walkway to the pet shop area of the yard. Shovel in the doorway. Next, clear out the store's floor by either shoveling, or you and your children can simply walk around packing down and smoothing the floor. Your children should then begin to work together deciding where each animal's area will be. They'll need to designate a fish tank section of the store, bird sanctuary, puppy and kitty kennels and a nice toasty tank for the iguana. If your children's stuffed animal collection does not include exotic beasts like iguanas and larakeets your children can easily craft them out of the snow. Once the animals are in their designated area of the store they will each need a food dish, shaped from snow, complete with favorite food, which just happens to be…snow! The animals will need little toys, like balls and bones, to play with. After getting the animals all arranged a cashier's corner will need to be created. Now, the shopping can begin. Your children will likely take turns role playing the lucky customer who gets to take a new animals home as well as the happy pet shop owner who gets to care for all the animals. Customers will come and go all afternoon looking, playing and buying new pets from the pet store.

SPRING

For the Birds

Materials: plastic netting bag, hairbrush, strings and grasses from around the yard

If you've ever been lucky enough to have a mother bird choose to build a nest for her young ones just outside your child's bedroom window you know first hand how incredible it is to watch a bird raise its young. You might question mother bird's ability to pick a quiet, restful location for her homestead but that's another story. Your child can get a hand in this excitement by helping Mother Bird in the building phase of her nest. Early in the spring when birds begin coming back to your area is prime time for this project. You'll need a bag made of plastic netting material. The plastic netting bags that hold onions in the grocery store work really well (when emptied). Have your child take the bag of netting and fill it up with things she finds in the yard that are soft, long and flexible. Grasses, long pine needles and soft, pliable twigs from the yard work very well. You can clean your child's hairbrush and she can add the soft hairs to the bag. If your child is able, give her a tape measure and some colorful yarn. She can cut strips of soft yarn about 6 inches long and stuff them in the bag as well. When the bag is full of nest building materials help her hang it from a tree branch that can easily been seen from an area where your child often plays or eats meals. It shouldn't take long and she'll find birds stopping by the "Nest Building Supply Store" for a one stop shopping experience of supplies. Remind her of the nice, soft materials she provided to help the mother bird make a cozy nest for the new, little babies. Later in the spring your child will discover nests around the neighborhood with the colorful string she cut and her soft hair keeping the baby birds warm. Can't say much for the therapeutic value of the onion aroma the nests may take on. Guess the birds will have to take that up with the complaint department.

Smell Off

Materials: 10 brown paper lunch bags, flowers and other aromatic finds from the yard

After surviving a winter of closed windows and frozen ground there's not much that beats the smell of spring time. That's about the only time I'd opt for the smell of warm dirt wafting through open windows over the smell of freshly baked chocolate chip cookies. Choose a day when your yard is springing to life with all kinds of aromatic fun finds, such as dandelions, sassafras leaves, pine branches, clover, grass, moist dirt, etc. Give your child 10 brown paper lunch bags. Tell her you two are going to have a smell off. That'll be sure to intrigue the young child's mind. She should go smelling into the yard to play this game. First, she must smell all over the place without picking anything. The point is to simply observe what things she finds that might surprise her with their smell? Is it a good smell? Is it yucky? Is it the neighbor's dog doo doo? Yipes! She may need to be a little critical with where she puts her sniffer. After she's sniffed all the new spring smells to be found, she should go back with her 10 brown bags and switch from sniffing to stuffing. All the things she found that had a good, strong smell go in a bag. One item for each bag. Instruct her to fold over the top and deliver the filled bag to a central location. When all 10 bags have been filled you close your eyes and it's your turn to sniff. Can you guess each item that she chose for a bag? What smells surprise you? Do you have a favorite? Do any smells trigger a certain memory? Share with her that the "smelling section" of the brain is right next to the "memory section" of the brain. Therefore, smells often trigger memories. In fact, you two might just be smelling up a memory right now. Make it another good one.

PROJECTS
FOR
ANYTIME

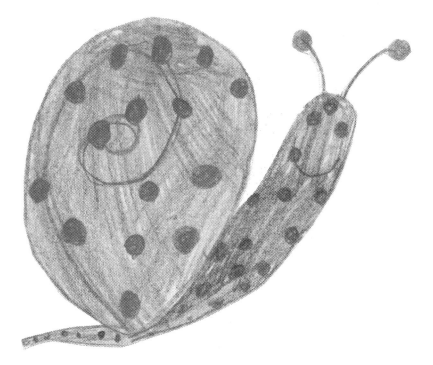

Nature Wristband/Bracelet

Materials: duct tape

Young children love collecting new things they find. Our three-year-old son's pockets are forever filled with goodies. I've found stones, pine cones, sticks, even a hostage ladybug. I'm trying to prepare myself for the day I find a frog in the pocket of his pants in the laundry. This activity will help your child collect fun finds in a new way. Wrap about 8 inches of duct tape around your child's non-dominant wrist. The tape must be placed sticky side up. If the temperature outside requires long sleeves or a coat be sure to place the tape over the sleeves so your child doesn't return with one icy, blue, decked out arm. He is now ready to explore the outdoors to decorate his wristband/bracelet with anything and everything he can find (bugs and frogs not included please). Any item deemed worthy gets stuck on to his wrist band. When completed, give praise for your child's workmanship. Carefully cut the wristband off the wrist and proudly display his design on the refrigerator for a few days (positive reinforcement for his outdoor, independent accomplishment will help build excitement for playing again the future. Despite what you may see at times, children are very motivated to please their parents). If your child really gets into this activity, get creative. Make two wristbands, a couple of leg warmers and a tie. Might want to forego the headband, too difficult to explain the strange new hair pattern to the stylist.

Variation: Challenge older children to use discretion when searching throughout the yard. Encourage your child to use smaller objects on his wristband and to create his design using a pattern such as ABBA (pine needle, flower, flower, pine needle, etc.). Pattern building is a great beginner math skill for your child to practice.

Color Hunt

Materials: markers, empty egg carton

Egg cartons provide yet another novel way for your young children to store collectables they find in the yard. The shape of the egg carton lends itself nicely to sorting which is another important elementary math skill. Once your family has eaten their way through a dozen eggs (not recommended in one sitting) wash and dry the egg carton. Instruct your child to color the "cubby" of each egg compartment a different color using his washable markers. The task will then be to go hunting outside for one or two items of each color and fit them into the corresponding cubby (The second part of this is crucial if your child is in the literal phase of development. I overheard my three year old son excitedly telling his sister he was going to use Dad's Craftsman Chainsaw for the yellow cubby). When the cubbies are full take a few minutes to review together the colors that were found in the yard and proudly exclaim the job was well done. If you live in a seasonal area this activity is best in the spring, summer or fall. If attempted in the winter with snow on the ground there is a good likelihood your child may not make it back to the house proudly displaying the filled egg carton until next Tuesday. The yellows and blues are a challenge to run into in the middle of winter.

*note: if there is more than one child participating you may find it easiest to use one egg carton per child or prep them for teamwork and cooperation before they hit the trail. If you do hear disagreements between your children try to hold back from solving it for them. Give your children the opportunity to talk things out and find a compromise on their own. It can be difficult to watch your children struggle but these moments provide important life lessons for them to learn and grow from.

Anytime Egg Hunt

Materials: last year's empty Easter eggs, raisins

Think you can dig up last year's plastic Easter egg shells? Maybe you're one of those super organized parents with everything titled with a label-maker. One day I'll achieve that. For now, I think I can probably find two dozen or so of last year's shells hibernating in the back of the game closet sleeping quietly until next Easter. Haul those guys out and give them to your children with the instructions to fill each egg with two raisins, three sunflower seeds or some such healthy snack combination. When they've completed the job you'll need about three minutes while your children hide their faces somewhere inside the house. Head outside yourself and hide all the eggs throughout the yard. Essentially, your children are reliving the fun of the Easter Egg Hunt. Why save it for just once a year? They'll need a morning snack or afternoon snack anyway. Why not make them earn it outside? To avoid any hurt feelings if you've got more than one hunter, divide the number of eggs by the number of hunters. Instruct your children how many they can each find so they'll end with an even amount. If they seem to be enjoying themselves, they can refill the eggs and this time one child hides the eggs, one child seeks for them and you get caught up on bills and laundry. Win, win, win!

*variation: if your children are old enough, have one child hide the eggs in the yard right from the start while the other child is the seeker. Once the seeker has recovered all the eggs, the children can refill the empty eggs and switch roles on their own.

*one more thought: we use this activity quite often. Don't be shy about using any of these activities over and over again. If you've found a way to get your children playing happily outside come back to it often. You'll find that once your children are outside working on an activity, it's often a catalyst to continued play even when the activity is completed.

Read, Rest, Relax

Materials: leaf pile, bean bag or blanket nest, picture book or coloring book

So often when we think of children outdoors, we picture them running, sweating, jumping, digging and getting dirty. There's a good reason for that. It's what children do. Don't get me wrong. This is exactly what we want our children to do outdoors. There is, however, room for teaching children the good in simply enjoying quiet time outdoors. For some reason, this idea is often overlooked by both parents and children. Help situate your child in a cozy spot in the sun on a beautiful, warm, spring afternoon or the shade on a toasty, summer morning. To encourage your child to try some outdoor quiet time, create a nest of sorts for her. Rake up a beautiful pile of crisp fall leaves, bring out a favorite bean bag to get comfortable in or find a pile of stadium blankets to arrange with edges curled up or scrunched up. There are many ways to create a cozy circle of comfort around her. Help make her aware of the feeling of the warm sunshine and breeze, the smell of the leaves and dirt around her, and the sounds of the birds. Teach your child to be still and soak in the beauty around her. Place a picture book in the nest or a coloring book with supplies. Your child can sit for a little while with her eyes closed listening and feeling. She can then take some time to work on a quiet activity she might usually complete inside the house like reading a picture book or coloring. Most adults love a peaceful moment outside on a beautiful day, why wouldn't your child?

Going Up!

Materials: basket, long rope or craft yarn

Most young children get a charge out of sending and receiving secret messages. Well, for that matter, older children do as well. Just talk to a teen's parent about their text messaging bills! This creative play activity works best when played with at least two people. You'll need to find a basket with a handle, a sandbox bucket or some such container that can be attached to a long string and lifted without spilling its contents. Once you've found your container secure a rope about 20 feet long or a string of the same length to the handle of the bucket or basket and your children are ready to play. Your children will find the most success with this activity if you can find one spot in your yard that is elevated near a spot that is low. You might use a deck, a tree fort, or a second story patio. I wouldn't recommend sending a child to the roof of the house but your children will easily get into play with this if the two children are on different levels. Play starts with the child on the raised surface packing a surprise in the basket for the other child waiting on the ground. He might decide on using a special leaf, a flower, a cool stone, or anything that strikes him as a special surprise. He loads the basket and lowers it down using the rope. When the receiver gets the basket, she takes out the surprise and loads her own special find. After loading and unloading, raising and lowering goes on for a while your children can decide when it's time to take all the surprises and set up a store or museum exhibit displaying all the cool findings in the yard. If you have a structure in the yard for play such as a tree fort or climbing tower on a swing set, it's worth picking up a cheap pulley at a hardware store. When your children have a pulley as part of their regular play they are likely to experiment with physical concepts such as weight, force and drag. Finding as many ways as possible to mix learning with play is a great way to enrich your children's developmental years.

Hide and Seek

Materials: set of paper cups or any other items that can be personalized, craft supplies

Here's a new twist on an old classic. Turn 10 paper cups or paper plates upside-down in front of your children and ask them to transform the cups or plates into people using markers, construction paper, pipe cleaners, stickers or anything else you can dig out of the art tub. When they have the group of 10 people completed it's time for the games to begin. One child must hide himself somewhere that peeking is not an option for a given length of time. During this time the other child will run outside and hide all ten people throughout the yard. One stipulation we found pretty important was that the hider must place the cup people so that they can be spotted without having to move anything out of the way. You always need to be one step ahead of the smart alec who might try to bury his people two feet in the dirt for safe keeping. When given the "all clear" the seeker child runs outside to see how many paper cup people he can recover. Then switch the roles. The seeker becomes the hider and the hider becomes the seeker. When all cup people have been recovered don't be too surprised if your children begin to give these little people names and personalities. They are likely to begin playing creatively with them. Our children had a few of their paper cups married before the afternoon was through. I'm expecting little Dixie Cups to be running around the yard soon.

*variation: If you only have one child playing this game you may need to hide the cups and allow your child to seek. If you have more than two you may find it best to create teams or have the children take turns being the hider while everyone seeks.

Nature Picture

Materials: sketch of item of interest, glue stick, sturdy paper

Most young children latch on to some type of object and become fascinated by it. For some it is trains, it could be butterflies, jets, robots, princesses, you name it. The sky is the limit. Sometimes the object of the child's fascination is illogical. Our family doesn't live anywhere near the ocean, we have not visited the ocean in over three years yet our three year old son lives, breathes, talks, walks octopus. There's an octopus living at a local zoo but every time we've encountered him he refuses to budge. I will never know from where this fascination was born but here it is. Is your child fascinated by something as well? If not fascinated, is there something he enjoys looking at or thinking about? This activity needs to be personalized by you for your child. Sketch an outline of this object on a sheet of sturdy paper. With the sketch in one hand and glue stick in the other your child is prepared for an afternoon of exploration and expression. Have him find the right materials to fill each part of the sketch. Offer a few creative suggestions he might try. Perhaps an owl's eye would be recreated by an acorn cap and the feathers could be peeled off pine cone pieces. Our son's octopus arms were made from long grasses and the siphon was a small hollow stick found in the yard. Your child can use soil, sand, stems, sticks, stones, just leave the snails and slugs alone. When the artwork is completed rave to your artist about what a beautiful work of art he created. Find a spot to display the artwork proudly for a while (just keep the picture hanging over a flooring surface you can easily clean. These pieces of art seem to easily shed their outdoor goodies when someone sneezes too loudly).

Feed the Birds

Materials: bag of birdseed, brown paper lunch bag

There's something about taking care of animals that seems to speak to almost all children. Even the lowliest of goldfish can bring out the caretaker in children. If you've got a backyard, odds are pretty good you've got birds. Telling an active, young child to go outside to sit and watch the birds, listen to the birds, count the birds just seems to be, well, for the birds. Most children have too much spunk and energy for such a sedentary, open-ended task. Now, give a child a bag of bird seed and you've got a whole different story. I wouldn't pile a 15 pound bag into the arms of an eager three-year-old no matter how enthused he seems. Instead, scoop some bird seed about 1/3 full in a brown, paper lunch type bag. Give the bag to your young child and tell him the birds are hungry in the yard. You can hear it from their calls. They need your child's help. Let him wander the yard independently with his bag of bird seed and it won't take long for him to go into action. He will likely fill any bird feeder he can find in the yard. You will see him sprinkle bird seed all throughout the yard and he may even make little bird seed piles here and there. The beauty of it is from time to time, you'll see him stop and observe the birds that he is hearing and spotting flitting around the backyard. That's a great moment to set down the mixer; your banana bread can wait, and take a few minutes to talk with your child about the birds he's helping to take care of. What kinds of birds can you identify? Can you copy their calls? Then get back to your bread the let him continue feeding and observing the birds. Encourage him to sit quietly for just a few minutes after the feeding to watch the variety of birds coming and going enjoying the afternoon snack he served up for them.

Picto-Mystery

Materials: quick sketch of 8 landmarks in your yard on index cards, treasure in a bag

This activity requires a little extra effort but if you're a quick artist I think you can still get it set up in five minutes. Quickly draw eight, or so, major landmarks from your yard such as a tell tale tree, the hose, an air conditioner unit, storage barn, etc. on eight index cards. One landmark per card. Next, put a treasure, could be a favorite stuffed animal, sidewalk chalk, and a tape measure, anything that would motivate your child to continue creative play once discovered, in a brown lunch bag. Tell your children to sit tight for a minute while you go to prepare a surprise. No peeking allowed. I found it easiest to work this one backward. Place the treasure in a hiding spot somewhere in your yard. It should be one of the landmarks that you drew. Once the treasure has been stashed go to another one of the landmarks you drew and place the card depicting the landmark where the treasure is hidden. This will serve as a clue to your children where to head next in order to find the treasure. Now walk to another landmark you drew and place the index card of the landmark you were just at. Continue this process of working through your landmark cards placing a clue for your children of the previous landmark. You'll end with one last card. Go back inside to your children and inform them there has been a treasure placed somewhere in the yard. They must now use the clues to discover where the treasure is hidden and use it to play outside. Give them the last card you're holding which will serve as their first clue. If you didn't get befuddled along the way, they should be able to go from landmark to landmark finding each clue which leads them to the next clue. After sleuthing throughout the yard for a while they should be able to reach the treasure in the end and begin playing. Not only will they feel proud they have reached the reward, you can feel pretty brainy for setting the activity up successfully. If the clues got a little tangled, well, grab another cup of coffee and try again a little later in the afternoon.

Magical Message Mailbox

Materials: small metal mailbox

Many craft stores and even some large department stores sell small, metal replica mailboxes. These mini mailboxes come complete with the latching door and a little flag that raises and lowers. We have found these can be an invaluable resource for communicating with our children. Fasten one mailbox per child to a special spot in the yard. It's best if you can find a different, special spot for each child's mailbox. However, if you've got a family of seven kids you may just run out of space in the yard for all the mailboxes, and come to think of it, that's probably the least of your concerns. From time to time write out a note if your child is learning to read otherwise draw a picture and put that little "happy-gram" in your child's mailbox and raise the flag. Compliment her on something you noticed she did that she may have thought went unnoticed. Maybe she cleaned the bathroom without being asked...HA! Who am I kidding? A little more realistic? How about picking up her room without being asked. Give your son a little note about how proud you were when he helped his brother getting some tricky shoes on without being asked. You might put afternoon snacks in the mailbox. Put a few fun stickers in the mailbox and raise the flag so when your child comes home from the trip to the grocery store she can see she has mail! Tell your child that she can use the mailbox both ways. When she needs to send you a little note she can put her message in the mailbox and raise the flag. You'll find your children will also enjoy sending little "happy-grams" to each other as well. These mailboxes help remind each child that in all the hustle and bustle of life she is important, loved and always your joy.

Petal Picture

Materials: sturdy paper, glue, pencil

Ask your child to sketch a rough outline of a picture he likes to draw or a scene that makes him feel happy. He may only use one grey pencil to make this drawing. It's best if you are able to offer some paper that is sturdier than sketch pad paper or printer paper. That type doesn't stand up very well when weighted with loads of glue and a variety of petals from the yard attached to it. Construction paper will do the trick as well as tag board, poster board or even the cut out bottom of a shoe box. This pencil drawing will need to be brought to life with color. The color for your child's picture comes from the flowers he finds in the yard. When he has the sketch complete your child should take his picture outside and begin searching the yard for just the right colored flowers to add just the right color to his picture. For example, if there is a sunshine in his picture, the rays can be dandelion pedals glued onto the sunshine. If there is a dog in the picture, the fur can be Queen Anne's Lace petals. A dog's pink tongue can be made from one small phlox petal. Buttercups can make the yellow color for the bird in sky. A leash could be the dandelion stalk or a thin stick. Green grass on the ground can be green grass on the sketch, or better yet, something unique your child is able to think up and find. The fun of this project is for your artist to look at flowers in a new way and evaluate what might best be used to add life, color and dimension to the sketch. Encourage your child to think outside of the box and use his own new, innovative thoughts. When the picture is completed don't forget to exclaim how beautiful the artwork looks. Discuss how the final product compares with the original sketch. Tap into your child's creative side. It's fascinating to see how he expresses himself and his ideas.

Season Booklet

Materials: cardboard tube, area outdoors that displays seasons the best, crayons, paper, hard surface to write on

In your yard there is probably an area that reflects the changing of the seasons dramatically. A deciduous tree, a flowering bush, a vegetable garden or any other area that emulates the season would be perfect for this activity. Have each child decorate his or her own viewing scope. Paper towel tubes work really well. The viewing scope will be used to limit the view of their seasonal study specimen. With each scope decorated, gather up the other materials and head outside to your preselected seasonal specimen. Your children will look through their scope so that the view is focused primarily on the area of the yard you have preselected. Once they have got a good view of that area your children must start really observing what they see. In as great detail as they can your children will begin to draw what they see in their scope. Add the color to match what they see. When the page is finished it must be stored away until a time you notice a significant difference in that same outdoor area. At that point, your children can decorate a new scope and head out for the same area. Again, they draw what they see in the scope in this new season. Using color and as much detail as they can muster is important. Your children will be telling the story of this season through the page they are working on. As the seasons continue to change, repeat the process adding more pages to their individual books. When the year is complete each child should have about three or four pages showing how the seasons affect the specimen studied. Your children can create a title page and then staple the work together. Read the books together and talk a bit about why they think the changes may have happened. Predict what will happen next. It's also interesting to see how your children's ability to observe, record and draw improves over time.

Rock Show

Materials: stones, paints, old toothbrush

The true beauty in a stone is revealed when it is put through the painstaking process of a good polishing. Your child cannot be expected to polish a pile of stones to appreciate the beauty to be found within. Did you know, however, simply getting a stone wet can also reveal in great detail the lines, patterns and colors nearly as vividly as when polished? Have your child collect a pile of pebbles and stones either from the yard or on a nature hike you take together. At first this pile will look simply like a bland grouping of regular old rocks. Give your child an old toothbrush and a bucket of water. Ask her to scrub each stone clean and she'll watch as new details, colors and patterns reveal themselves. What at first was a pile of grey rocks now becomes beautiful stones showcasing hues of pink, browns, blues, white and even some with sparkles reflecting the sun's light. Your child can set all these cleaned stones in a safe place to dry and simply let them be part of a rock show. Have her come to show you her display. Which stone is her favorite? Can she remember which stone changed the most when made wet? Point out to her which stone you like the most and tell why. After a meaningful little talk about the stones your child may decide to set them out to be displayed for others to enjoy for a few days or she may see these stones as begging for her own ideas with color and personality. If that's the case, take out the paints, send her back outside and let her give each stone her own spin. Some stones may become little creatures or people. Other stones may be adorned with new patterns and beautiful colors. Let her look at each new stone and find the inspiration to put her own mark on them. When finished and dried, these new stones are ready for display. The small ones may even get a little magnet on the back and be promoted to the fascinating life of a refrigerator magnet!

Leaf Rubbing Book

Materials: five blank printer pages, stapler, leaves, crayon peeled of its wrapping

Present your child with a blank booklet you've made from five white printer papers folded in half and stapled together in the middle. Tell him today he will be creating a beautiful book about leaves. Each leaf will have its own special page. Demonstrate the method on the cover page for your child. Place a leaf on "page 2". Be sure to place the leaf smooth side down. The veins are most defined on the back of the leaf allowing for the most dramatic rubbing in color. Fold the cover paper over the leaf and hold it securely with your "helper hand" (non-dominant hand). Rub the long side of a peeled crayon lightly across the paper. You should see a beautiful print of the leaf appearing on the page. This is where you're hoping to get some "oooo"s and "ahhhhh"s from your audience. Now title the book to your child's liking and send your little artist into the great beyond, or at least the front and back yard, in search of just the right leaves for his book. To make the book even more interesting some children may want to vary the colors of each page or perhaps use several different colors on one leaf. Have fun and be creative. If your child collected small leaves he can fit more than one per page. To reinforce his independent outdoor effort it would be worth "reading" the book together at story time. Let your author describe where he found each leaf and why he decided to include it in his book. See if you can chime in with what kind of leaf it is. Make your seventh grade science teacher proud with the knowledge you've retained from that leaf collection you were forced into.

Memory Cards

Materials: stack of square papers cut from sturdy paper, glue

Most young children are familiar with the classic game of Memory. There are two identical stacks of cards which are laid face down in an organized way on a flat surface. Each player takes a turn flipping two cards over trying to make a match of the pictures or patterns on the face of the cards. The key to making matches is for players to remember the pattern on each card as well as the card's position. If a match is found the cards are withdrawn and placed in that player's "keeper pile". When all of the cards have been removed from play, the player with the most cards wins the game. This game is a great challenge for the young child's mind. She must sort the pictures and patterns in her mind to find the identical ones. At the same time, she must remember the placement of many cards in order to find a match. Instead of playing the game with a set of cards purchased from a store your child can make her own cards. Give your child a stack of perhaps ten squares of blank paper. The appropriate number of cards will depend on your child's age and ability to hang in there with a job independently. She will have to glue two matching items from nature on two separate cards. She may choose to use two maple leaves, two blades of grass, two flower petals, two pine needles, etc. When the set of cards has been completed and given some drying time decide together on a good spot outdoors to play the game together. As you turn cards over revealing new items chosen from the yard be sure to talk a little about each choice.

Nature Collage

Materials: the yard

You'll need to offer your young children some guidance to get this creative activity started. Walk together around the yard and find something unique that will get the your children's creative juices flowing. You might use the head of a daisy, a thistle, an empty bird's nest, anything that gets your children excited to start. Place this item in the center of your children's art construction area, which will need to be an open area free from obstacles. The challenge will be for each child to find new items they deem unique and place it with the existing objects so that the new piece interacts in some way with the original item. You might start the activity off with three daisy heads connecting so they look similar to gears. Now each child gets to take their turn in finding something they deem interesting from the yard to place with the original daisies in a creative way. Each child takes a turn to bring his or her item back to the art construction site and must find a way to connect the new item to the original structure. There's no right or wrong way to build this creation. It simply requires teamwork and creativity. Once your children get the concept of finding interesting items and creative ways to add them to the existing creation you are set to let them explore and create. The larger the construction gets the more creative your workers will become. They'll have fun picking up ideas from one another to build upon. Offer compliments and exclamations of pride as they get the activity started.

Sand Castle

Materials: buckets, shovels, plastic butter knife

Has it been raining all night? The swings are probably too wet for swinging and the slide will leave the slider's pants soaked through. Normally this type of morning might fall victim to the TV while your children wait for the world to dry up. No need. Did you know that your sandbox outside is in the perfect condition for constructing a beautiful sandcastle? Since it's not always possible to drive our children to the beach, a sand castle can be created right at home under the perfect conditions. Clear all the toys out of the sandbox to create a clean, flat area of sand to work with. If it's a little chilly out dress your child in nylon wind pants and let them sit on a plastic grocery bag or garbage bag to keep out the cold moisture. If it's warm enough, shorts are perfect. Demonstrate how tipping a bucketful of wet sand can create a castle tower. Plastic butter knives can carve steps to the high towers or poke little windows for the king and queen to peer out from. Even young children can create fanciful trees to dot the kingdom by using the "drizzle" method. Fill a bucket about 2/3 full of sand and then top it off with water from the garden hose. Show your child how to pick up a fist full of sand and let the watery sand slowly drizzle through your fingers. Drop all the watery sand in a pile on top of itself and you'll create a magical looking tree for the castle grounds. Your child will be constructing towers and growing trees all morning and before you know it, the grass will be dry enough to run and play in.

*variation: if you do not have a sandbox a temporary one can be created for the yard using a large, plastic storage type of tub. Simply fill the tub with sand to a level your child can comfortably reach in and work with. If you haven't had rain in a while you can easily remedy this by squirting the sandbox with water from the garden hose for a few minutes to give it a good soaking. Who needs beachfront property when you've got a tub of wet sand? (OK, put your hand down. I know the tub doesn't hold a candle to the beach but it's a close second.)

Woodland Cottage

Materials: milk jug belt (see page 30 for milk jug belt instructions)

Children are often intrigued by all things miniature. Making a miniature woodland cottage or fairy house is very enchanting. If you happen to live in the middle of a national forest you're children probably have all the building supplies they could hope for. However, if you reside in suburbia like much of America does you may need to embark on a field trip to gather the variety of supplies needed for your child to create a magical woodland cottage. Strap your constructor into the ole' milk jug belt (classy looking thing isn't it?) and trek off to a county park, hiking path or nearby woods. One of the most essential pieces to collect is moss. The more varieties of moss your child can find the better. Moss will provide the carpeting in the cottage and if your child is bent toward the seventies maybe even enough leftover for a little shag on the walls. Try to find flowers that tilt downward for a floor lamp. Lilies of the Valley, Japanese Lanterns or Foxgloves work great. You'll need four sticks in the shape of a Y for both ends of each wall to provide the frame for the cottage. Your child will need interesting sticks to provide the coverage of the walls. Pine branches do very well as the walls of the cottage. Point out ideas to your child and accept all of his ideas. Be careful not to put your ideas in place of his. If he wants an acorn to be a monster truck in the garage, be all about it. Once the milk jug is brimming with building supplies and your child's head is filled with the building plans you are ready to let him at it. Once home, encourage him to work from the ground up. Lay the carpeting first. For the walls, poke the four Y sticks in the ground at each corner of the house. Lay a stick resting in the valley of two Y sticks and now your child can begin setting other sticks against the long stick in order to create walls. Once the basics are in place he can start decorating with doo dads. Remind your child that he should also roam the yard to see what might be found to perfect his woodland cottage. Take a picture of his handiwork when finished. A woodland cottage this innovative ought to be preserved forever.

Outdoor Stew

Materials: old pot, ladle

For better or worse, children love to help cook. Despite how the family chef may feel, it is great for children to get involved in the kitchen. The conversations and experiences regarding measurements, ingredients, cooking times, even chemical reactions like the effects of baking soda and baking powder all help widen their knowledge base and believe it or not their science and math skills as well. There is another kind of cooking that kids should get to experience. That is outdoor, creative cooking. Given an old pot to use and a ladle to serve up their cuisine, children's imagination will run wild when headed outdoors to whip up a pot full of their delight. No matter the season there are more ingredients outside for your children to cook with than you can probably find in your own kitchen pantry. Without being told what to do or given a recipe to follow your children will start grabbing a few handfuls of grass, sprinkling in some sand and dirt, plucking a nice, ripe leaf and topping it all off with some acorns, pinecones and crushed sticks (you can never have too much fiber, right?). What could be better? If you've got more than one chef involved have them serve up a bowl for the other to enjoy. They may even decide to hold their own recipe exchange. A few important rules of thumb your children should be aware of; make sure each child clearly understands this cooking is for pretend. It is never alright to eat things from outside without a parent or trusted adult's permission. Secondly, if it's winter be sure your chefs leave the yellow snow for the next guy's stew.

A PROP
+
A STORY
= PLAY

Pirates of the Backyard

Materials: ribbon, paper, bandanas, empty paper towel tube, crumpled ball of aluminum foil

Sometimes when a child looks out at a yard and simply sees an expanse of grass and nothing more he may need a little help getting his creative engines fired up. A scenario or storyline and a few simple props are often all it takes to get the play started in your child. Many children are intrigued by any storyline having to do with pirates, at least the romanticized type. The prospect of buried treasures and ships is irresistible. For each child participating, cut a paper triangle large enough to cover his eye. Cut two small slits near the upper corners of the eye patch and weave a ribbon, cut about 18 inches long, through the slits. Tie the eye patches to each pirate's head. Beware, humans get their depth perception ability from binocular cues, or input from both eyes. If you see your child is running into trees and house corners you may need to interfere in play for a moment for safety's sake and lift the flap on the eye patch restoring his ability to perceive distances correctly. No one needs a pirate with a goose egg on his forehead. If you have bandanas in the house put one on each pirate's head as well. Give your pirate a telescope, otherwise known as a paper towel tube, and bring them to their pirate cove. Each pirate will need an assigned area to guard against oncoming pirates. Use the telescope to see if the ships coming by (cars on the street driving by) are friendly or appear to be aggressive in which case defense measures must be taken. While you are escorting your band of pirates throughout the yard explaining how this creative play gets started, stealthily drop balls of silver treasure, a.k.a. pre-rolled aluminum foil balls, throughout the yard. Instruct the pirates that there is the same number of treasures per pirate. With the prospect of oncoming enemies, hidden treasures and simple props, why, "shiver me timbers," your little maties are in for an afternoon of fun in the sun.

Movie Extension

Materials: movie, simple prop

Creative outdoor play is not unlike creative writing. Sometimes writers are given a blank sheet of paper and see nothing but potential. The story begins to flow and creative juices are nearly unstoppable. At other times, that same creative writer looks at a sheet of white paper and sees just that, a blank sheet of white paper. No ideas come to mind. Children can be the same when it comes to creative play. Sometimes their minds drum up amazing ideas for creative play. Play goes deep and they get lost in their imaginary world. Other times, you open the door to send them outside to play and they stand there staring blankly at a yard full of grass. No creative play ideas come to mind. Writer's block of sorts. This is all very normal and you will be able to help your child through this.

From time to time, caregivers choose to show children a movie. The conclusion of a movie is the perfect time for a child to begin creative, outdoor play. They have been given characters they now identify with and have build up empathy for, a setting they've watched from many perspectives and were just brought through a terrific plot. Give your children a simple prop such as a magic wand, a bandana, a necklace, or pass out a paper plate for them to turn into a mask or hat to help identify themselves as the character they are about to become. Help the child fall into character with an accent or other telltale character trait. Detail the yard together as the elements of the setting from the story. Your characters can play either a repeat of what they watched or better yet create the sequel to the story. Once you can hear the excitement is building and the creative engines are firing, let your children begin their independent play outside and watch the afternoon melt away in an imaginary, outdoor world. You will know this is a success when your children have played creatively outdoors for a longer period of time than it took to watch the movie.

Treasure Hunt

Materials: shoe box covered in aluminum foil, treasure map, items to initiate creative play

Who can resist the magic of a buried treasure? Time to work up some magic for your children. Crudely wrap a shoe box or other similar sized container in aluminum foil. I say crudely because it is very likely to soon be torn apart in the discovery phase anyway. What to pack in the shoebox, however, you should put more effort into. The purpose of this creative play activity is to bring out imaginative, innovative thought in your child. If you simply pack in a snack or a token toy as a "prize" your child will follow the map, find the buried treasure and the fun in over in all of seven minutes. Remember what you are trying to accomplish is using a novelty item or group of items to initiate creative play. What you pack in the treasure chest is dependent on the interest of your child and the number of children involved. Perhaps you might pack a rope, a small bucket and a shovel, and that will spark your child's imagination. Find some sort of combination that is most likely to stir up some sort of intriguing play in your child. Could it be a magnifying glass, pencil and paper? A small truck to be played with outdoors and some sort of collapsible ramp? My mom used to tell me "a little goes a long way". I have found that a little creativity from the planner goes a long way in creating quality episodes of play in the children. Once you have packed the treasure chest, secretly bury it somewhere in the yard. You might decide to up the ante and hide it under some leaves or camouflage it with a earth tone towel. Sketch out a crude map showing your house and yard from a bird's eye view. Add a dotted walking trail to be followed by your treasure hunters. Don't forget the big red "X" that marks the spot. Scroll roll the treasure map by rolling both ends to the middle and present the secret, treasure map to your hunters who by now can't wait to get outside and play. Now, isn't there a treasure of sorts waiting for you in the laundry room?

Little People

Materials: poster putty or play dough, pen, milk jug belt (see page 30 for milk jug belt instructions)

Toy companies know what they are doing when they manufacture a set of little figurine people. They have teams of people who have researched scads of children and know that kids love to imagine, pretend and impersonate. Rather than going out to purchase the newest set of little figurine people, your children can make their own little guys and will probably be more proud and love these little people more than those purchased from a store. We found that poster putty works the best for this activity but in a pinch play dough works too. Bear in mind, this could mean be the end of the road for that play dough chunk. The play dough doesn't fare too well in the spaghetti noodle maker with little sticks, leaves and dirt throughout. Start by showing your children an example of a little person they can make by using an acorn, a pebble or a pine cone as a body. Slap on some poster putty and give your little fella some arms, legs, and a hat using sticks and little leaves. Next draw on a face and you've got yourself a fine looking little gentleman. Encourage your child to make a friend for this little guy in the same fashion. Strap on the milk jug belt and have your children scour the yard collecting all the necessary body parts. They'll come back with little sticks, stones, pine cones, flowers for dresses and a smattering of other creative goodies. Each child should unload his jug so all supplies are at the ready as construction is under way. Set out little globs of poster puddy or play dough and watch your children get to work. Before you know it, your intent little workers will create a whole family of five for that original little fella complete with a pet dog! Your children can make a home for this family under a tree, in a bush or wherever their imagination takes them. 50 bucks says that is not the last time your children will ask to play with these little people outside.

Ribbon Dance

Materials: outdoor music, a stick, at least one if not several long ribbons

The novelty of music outdoors can be enough to intrigue almost anyone. Set up some music outdoors. Then ask your child to go hunting for a smooth, strong stick while you dig out some ribbon or craft yarn. Tie the ribbon to one end of the stick and let a good length of ribbon, perhaps three to four feet, hang down. If your child has any clothes she enjoys dressing up in that can also be used outdoors send her off to the dress up trunk. Start the music and let that little dancer go. Your child will likely not need to be instructed on the correct ribbon dance technique. Children have lovely, vivid imaginations. It will be fun to allow her creativity and expression come to life. Even if you are up to your elbows in chicken trying to pound out some cor don bleu, try to stop a moment, go outside (no watching through the window) to praise the performance. Giving a child positive attention for the way she has expressed herself is so vital to the healthy development of a child. If she seems to be enjoying herself ask her to create a routine. Keep that child spinning and creating all afternoon.

Why play music in any outdoor, creative playtime?

There has been a good deal of research in the area of music and the way it impacts young children. Music has been found to be motivating while also calming and relaxing to those listening. Children's heart rates have been found to drop a bit when music is played, particularly so when nature sounds are included. Music is processed in both hemispheres of the brain therefore stimulating the entire brain which enhances learning. Studies have found that subjects felt higher levels of joy and play occurred more "naturally and frequently" (American Music Therapy Association, Inc). Well, if that doesn't make the case for playing music while your children play I don't know what does. While your children are playing outdoors they are already experiencing the sounds of nature. Add some music to outdoor play and watch the level of creativity go up and well as the duration of each play episode. So, pump up the jam.

Boxes of Fun

Materials: empty box

Never, ever, under ANY circumstances throw away a perfectly good, clean, empty box, EVEN if it's recycling tomorrow, without first squeezing all the play possible out of that old thing. You might be surprised to find out how much play is packed inside an empty box for your creative children. Keep this mantra in mind; the bigger the box the better. An empty refrigerator box will bring your kids a good couple weeks of play. When I was a child I think our family only needed a new refridgerator once. I have no idea anymore about the cool features of our new fridge, however, I can easily recall the fantasic space ship it was delivered in. Now, mind you, this refrigerator came in a brown, cardboard box like any other kitchen appliance but my brother and I immediately saw our new spaceship hovering down to the driveway when the new fridge came. My mom couldn't wait to get her hands on the fridge and we couldn't have been happier with our new box. Your children are no different. However, I'm not wishing a broken down refrigerator on you frequently enough to get good boxes. One bad fridge is enough in a lifetime. Good, large boxes are hard to come by. When your household does get a large box bring it outside with a set of markers. In true Pied Piper fashion your children are sure to follow. It's very likely your children will need no more than that. Set the box in a comfortable spot outside in the yard and back away. You'll watch your children walk around the box, touch it a bit, and turn it around. They're sizing it up and getting the creative gears churning. Soon you've got kids decorating, designing, working together, resolving conflict, compromising, and best of all transporting themselves to a new time and place. If your children are able to independently squeeze a good amount of play from an empty box, congratulate yourself. They are being given a childhood that's promoting creativity, independence, team work skills and self-confidence. Don't look now but those skills are vital to success later in life.

Welcome to the Jungle

Materials: brown, paper grocery bags, bananas, tape

Many children are intrigued by monkeys and their silly antics. One will quickly come to this conclusion by strolling a zoo and listening to the thrilling sounds coming from the children being entertained by a troupe of goofy monkeys. Both sets of creatures tend to enjoy hanging around, showing off and just plain old being silly. Surprise your young children by setting up a rainforest in the yard and challenging them to search out their own bananas to enjoy for a snack. To create the props for the rainforest rip brown, paper grocery bags into long strips. Start at the opening on one side of the paper bag and rip a section about 6 inches wide. Rip the paper down the side of the bag, across the bottom and up the other side. Continue to rip approximately two more strips from that bag. Tape or staple the three strips together. Next, twist the brown, stapled, paper strip from the top to the bottom so you've created a nice looking tropical vine. Complete as many vines as you feel will intrigue your children and stir up some creative, imaginative play. Tape or otherwise attach the vines in the area of the yard where the rainforest play will be. After attaching the vines hide one banana per monkey in the yard. Now send your monkeys out to "swing" from the vines and search out the bananas for a snack.

*interesting fact worth noting: rainforests take up less than 2% of the earth's surface but are home to nearly half of all life on our earth. It's well worth all efforts to reduce, reuse and recycle.

Costumes

Materials: old Halloween costumes

Sometimes creative play just needs a simple novelty item to provide a boost of energy and creativity. Halloween costumes can really pack a punch. If you see your child wandering the yard with that "nothing to do" look on her face, go grab that tub with Halloween décor and costumes and dig out an old, favorite costume. Your child probably only gets to wear this costume once a year and odds are it is a character she loves (unless she's stuck wearing the hand-me-down Indian costume that I wore, and my two younger sisters then wore. That old thing is probably floating around somewhere in the world of toss off costumes). Get that costume out in the middle of June and you'll be bringing about some creative magic. By simply changing or adding to what your child is wearing you can change her entire world, at least for the afternoon. I'm always amazed at what children are able to drum up when they are dressed as someone or something else. While you're helping your children get into their costumes ask them to describe what they see outside. You may need to help them come up with the first few ideas. For example, if you're getting Spiderman dressed up, do you see that dog on top of the swing set that needs saving? Getting a woodland fairy ready? I see all kinds of pretty dandelions that are needed in the oak tree bark to help bring about summertime to the land. Got a cat in costume? Warn them of the neighbor dog prowling around the neighborhood and put a bowl of cat pretzels outside for her to eat before the dog gobbles it up. You'll be pleasantly surprised at what creative ideas the two of you can come up with to get the ball rolling. Costumes work well for scoring candy on Halloween but I think using them as a catalyst for transforming a child's world for creative outdoor play isn't too bad either.

Tenting It

Materials: old sheets, clothes pins or other clips, patio furniture

Remember building a fort from a sheet? Or did you ever used to hide out under the dining room table (as a child that is, not last week after your daughter's cup of milk spilled on the carpet for the third time)? Children love to have little cubby spaces to play and designate as their own hiding spot. Take a few minutes to look at your yard and see where you could best attach a sheet to create such a nook for your child. Is there a low hanging branch you could fold a sheet over creating a traditional, triangular tent? Can you push yourself to get more creative? Do you have a chair you could place in the yard for the afternoon? Clip a sheet to the back of the chair and drape the other end to a tree branch. Never anchor a sheet to a chair or structure that is off the ground with a rock or other heavy object. Someone will surely have a goose egg on their forehead rendering the fun over immediately. Better to take a wayward clothes pin to the forehead than an unforgiving cinder block. Use your child's creative advice to help construct a really great backyard tent. Use two sheets if you've got two kids playing. As they are playing you'll hear them creating an entire neighborhood and popping here and there for visits or appointments. Hours of fun can be had from simply utilizing a sheet and some clips in a new way.

*word of caution: if you get carried away and put up too many tents in your backyard your neighbor is likely to show up touting his guitar and a few bongos thinking you're remaking Woodstock.

Walking on Air

Materials: craft yarn, shoes

This creative play idea is weird, I'll readily admit that. But for how odd and simple it is, it works amazingly well in initiating creative play. It's ridiculously easy to set up and is, in fact, simply that, ridiculous. Give it a shot. For this afternoon of fun you'll need to find a branch or stretch of lumber up high from which you can hang a string with clear space below for your children to play and experiment. We used a big, oak branch that hangs about 20 feet above our backyard. You could use a second floor deck railing or a swing set bar (although keep in mind the higher the better). Tie the end of a ball of yarn to the shoelaces on a pair of your child's shoe. Throw the shoe up and over the branch and it'll come falling back down to you. At this point in set up I had a squirrel reaming me out for entering his territory. If this happens to you as well never you mind him. It's a small sacrifice to pay in the name of great fun for your children. Let the shoe hang about ½ foot to a foot off the ground (any higher than that and the shoe will start kicking your kids in the behind once it gets swinging. We learned that the hard way). Now cut the string and tie the loose ends to the same spot of the shoe. Essentially you are creating a pendulum of sorts. Give the shoe a good push and watch the pendulum in action. Now repeat this with several other shoes. Crazy how something so simple can be so fun. These shoes will become swings for favorite little buddies and moving obstacles in an obstacle course. Your children will even practice at playing catch with just themselves and their shoes. Swing one shoe at a ninety degree angle from another shoe. Your children will compare the rate of each shoe swinging and the screaming gets louder the closer the timing gets while the spectators anticipate the shoes intertwining. Watch your child use their shoes in innovative, creative ways that you never thought possible. Get Dad's big shoe out there on a string to act as a big bus for a slew of figurines. My apologies ahead of time if Strawberry Shortcake ends up smelling more like a sweaty sock than a basket of berries.

Vacation Package

Materials: form of luggage that can be dragged across the yard, chairs

Ever give your child the opportunity to pack before going on a trip? Hopefully you had the foresight to look over the luggage before leaving for your destination. I've seen suitcases packed with 8 pairs of socks, a train engine, some band-aides, and a beach shovel. Who needs a clean change of underwear when you're having fun, right? Well, better save the trip planning for the parents for now. However, this outdoor activity gives your child the power to plan and pack for his own vacation. Set up a couple of chairs outside in a row. These will simulate an airplane. Find some sort of bag that will pass for luggage. Got your grandpa's old, bowling ball bag stowed away in the basement from back in the day when you thought you might pick up bowling as a hobby? Well, now you have a legitimate use for that thing. Anything that will pass for luggage will do. Have your child talk about where in the world he might like to vacation. Could it be Antarctica? The Egyptian Pyramids? The Amazon River? Once the destination has been chosen he should pack his "suitcase" accordingly. Don't forget to stash away a little baggie of snack. Not to worry, drink boxes can get passed this security. Seat him on the plane and wave goodbye as the jet disappears into the clouds. This is the part when you disappear into the house to put things in order and try to get a few things done. Now your child's imagination and the contents of his suitcase will take over. If more than one child is partaking in this activity they will enjoy seeing what the other passenger has packed along for the journey. When the plane lands you'll see your explorers embarking on their adventure using the contents of their suitcases. Now, I apologize if you look out the window only to see eight pairs of perfectly clean, Sunday socks filled with sand and stones and tied around sticks. It might be a good idea to run the luggage through the security desk before the flight takes off. When the trip is over the suitcases must be unpacked and put away by the travelers. Ask your children about the things they saw while on their vacation. You'll enjoy hearing their tales while you all munch some of the bran muffins you just got done baking in your free time.

Clowning Around

Materials: broom, bikes, balls, books

Who doesn't like being entertained at the circus? Well, if watching the circus is so much fun, imagine performing in the circus! For the afternoon, think of your yard as a circus with stations. Your little clowns can move through the stations in the yard stirring up all sorts of silly ruckus. Have them dress up in silly clothes while you go outside to set up the simple stations. Stop one is walking the tightrope. What's a circus without a tightrope walk? Lay a broom on the ground or set each end of the stick on two very slightly elevated flat spots for your clowns to perform the death defying tightrope walk. The next stop is taking the clowns' bikes out and letting them drive in circles in the driveway. They can try simple, funny tricks like coasting with their legs sticking out straight all the while ringing their bells and honking horns. The third station involves your children in a balancing act while having a ball. Set out a few soft, playground type balls you may have in the garage and a few of those old, hardcover cookbooks you meant to cook decedent meals from and now you're surviving off hot dogs and mac and cheese. Good news! Your clowns can make great use of those books and it's got nothing to do with you messing around with Gouda stuffed manicotti! Your children can to try to balance the books on their heads while kicking the playground balls. This, by the way, we found provides some great Kodak moments. Do you have swings in your yard? Make the acrobatic clowns stop next at the swing station. Is there a tree they can climb safely? Look around your yard for any other clowning around stations you can create. Much like a kindergarten teacher would, explain to your nutty clown posse what fun is awaiting them at each station. When you've walked them through their circus, let the play begin. As any good ringmaster would, get the show started by bellering the traditional, "Ladies and Gentlemen, Children of all ages, welcome to the greatest show on earth!" (How about that for setting the bar high?)

Dinosaur Park

Materials: plastic figurines or other favorite set of toys

Sometimes by simply taking an old, favorite set of toys and moving them to a new location with some new props you have helped your child open up a whole new world of play with the same old toys. Can you help your child rustle up a pile of stones or rocks from the yard? Be careful here. I had to talk to my son about thievery after I found him searching out more fantastic stones by picking through the neighbor's landscaping. No worries, Mr. Cliff, we put them all back. Before you create a neighborhood Dennis the Menace help your child set up the new stone world as well as an understanding of property lines and limited resources. Stones packed together create an excellent backdrop for a prehistoric storyline. Once the new land has been created your child and his imagination will take over. Dinosaurs will roam this new earth in search of food and making friends. The mighty T-Rex is likely to "Roar" up from the rocks and try to foil the plans of the mighty Allosaurus. You'll soon hear your child narrating the storyline, which by the way is an excellent pre-writing strategy for later in his school career. He may add little props of his own like trees standing between the rocks to help hide the prowling T-Rex or sticks to be used as tools of defense. Your child's brain will jump into action by simply finding a new backdrop for an old toy. If you don't have a set of dinosaurs handy, any group of plastic figurines will do. Barbie may be making her away across the desert because she heard Macy's is having a sale. Cars and trucks might roar their engines trying to pass through the rough terrain. Perhaps aliens landed on earth and now must make their way through the barren land in search of human life. You know your child and how to spark that creative mind. Grab a favorite old set of toys and bring it to life on the rocks.

Outta This World

Materials: bike helmet, aluminum foil, toilet paper tube

3…2….1…Blast Off! To the backyard at least. Send your little explorer to the moon for the afternoon. Before heading out she'll first need her astronaut space suit to protect her from the harsh environment in space. There is virtually no air pressure in space which would cause an astronaut's unprotected body fluids to bubble and fizz. The space suits trap air pressure inside so the astronaut's body can function normally. And your son thought HE got in trouble for ripping a hole in his good pants. YIPES! Probably a little graphic for the very young but you might water the information down if you have a curious space cadet on your hands. A nice NASA space suit will set you back about $12,000,000 and weighs about 120 lbs. Probably not in the cards for play clothes. Aluminum foil, not NASA recommended by the way, sets you back about a buck ninety and weighs merely a few ounces. So to get your child geared up for an afternoon of outer space fun, wrap strips of aluminum foil around your child's legs and the tops of her arms. Put her bike helmet on her head as part of her outer space gear. She'll need a viewing device, otherwise known as a toilet paper tube, to help her scan the foreign surface of the moon. Bring your child out to her space craft. Anything can serve as a great spacecraft by the way. It could be the sandbox, swing set, particular tree she can sit in. You name it. The control tower is not picky. Now count down with your child from 10. Be sure your child counts down with you or repeats the numbers after you. This is a great teachable moment for number review. Now wave your good-byes. Your child is off for an afternoon of adventure on the moon.

*snack idea: for a little mid-afternoon energy snack mix a glob of peanut butter with a handful of oatmeal and squeeze some honey on top. Mush it all together and roll these "moon cookies" into little balls. No need to bake. Simply go on a moon walk of your own bearing Moon Cookies for your astronauts.

Buddy System

Materials: stuffed animal or doll that has never "played" outside before

Sometimes the novelty of something new breathes life into something once thought of as old. Hand your child a stuffed animal or doll that has never been given the privilege of exploring the world outside. Help your child get this activity started by telling him that his "Tommy" the stuffed turtle would love to be taught how to climb a tree. Just giving the imagination a jump start like this can often be enough to spring board a young child into a whole new world. Soon "Tommy" is happily shimmying his way up the backyard maple tree outside and proudly perching on a branch munching a few green leaves. Don't be surprised to hear your child chattering away at "Tommy" telling him how to climb trees, how to steer clear of bees and where the band-aids may be found if the need arises. Soon you may find that "Tommy" is now tucked under your child's arm being dragged all about getting the toddler tour of the yard. This type of creative, outdoor play is what transports your child to a world of imaginary fun and helps build independent confidence and creativity.

Parade Day!

Materials: outdoor music, instruments of any sort, popcorn

Everybody loves a parade. I would imagine even Ebenezer Scrooge with all his bad attitude would have leaned forward a bit to glance out the office window as a parade went marching by. Children especially cannot get enough of all the excitement and hoopla that surrounds a parade. The music, uniforms, floats, balloons and food adds to all the excitement. So, make it parade day in the yard! Let your children dress up for their parade appearance. Find whatever musical instruments you may have in the house. Better yet have your children make their own from oatmeal container drums to pan lid cymbals (neighbor dogs love that one), the old standby paper plate tambourine or by simply giving them two sticks to bang together in a pinch. Every now and again we have been to a parade where candy and other little trinkets are tossed out to the happy spectators. This parade just so happens to be one of those. While random candy tossing into a parade crowd can cause a feeding frenzy at the drop sight, we won't anticipate that sort of trauma at today's parade. Pop up a nice, big bowl of popcorn for the participants to pass out to the spectators, imaginary throngs of people or squirrels as the case may be, lining the streets. Pump up some outdoor music that has a lively beat. This will give the parade a special boost. Most children don't play very frequently with music floating through the yard. The novelty of music and energy from the beat will add a little fuel to their imagination. Push play and let the parade and popcorn passing begin. Don't be too concerned about the popcorn in the grass. After our children's parade ended it took a matter of about two hours and the squirrels had happily cleaned up the parade route. Not too sure the sodium intake did much good for the squirrels' blood pressure but they sure looked satisfied.

Super Heroes

Materials: towel or spare pillowcase, stuffed animals

If you listen to children who are able to sustain independent, creative play they will tell you they imagined a storyline that included some sort of problem that needed a resolution. This is really very similar to a good book or movie. When you have characters, a problem and a solution you have the building blocks for a good story or some great, creative play. You can tailor creative play storylines for your child based on her interest. Super Heroes offer a very simple, satisfying storyline for creative play. Many children enjoy the feeling of saving the world, or more realistically, finding a lost toy the family is turning the house upside-down looking for. Although the way your child may retell the story of recovering the misplaced toy you might think she had just lended her services and saved the world. Before notifying the United Nations regarding this act of selfless heroism have your child avert a few more catastrophes in the yard. Toss about ten stuffed animals or dolls in a bag. Head outside together with your child to get her started in setting the stuffed animals or dolls in positions that call for the help of no one else but…Super Hero! You might set one doll so that she will be stuck in the branches of a tree, another trapped under a bench. One stuffed bear might find itself upside down, ensnared in the hose hanger. Build the suspense while you and your child continue getting animals and dolls into precarious positions. Once the yard is in utter ciaos help your child suit up to come to the rescue. By simply tying a towel or spare pillowcase loosely around her neck you've transformed your young child into a super hero. She may even complete her costume with her own name. With a leap and a bound send her out into the world to fix all the problems she may encounter. Once all the little buddies have been saved she can set them all about the yard again in dire straights. Back again to saving the little helpless creatures. Talk about job security! Now you can go be a super hero and clean out that litter box.

Tea Party

Materials: outdoor table and chair for each child, tablecloth of sorts, tableware, snacks

Another way to help a child create and sustain creative, outdoor play is to introduce anything different or unique that will be seen as intriguing to your children. Admittedly, most of us adults can feel our curiosity piqued when there's something new to see or experience. Try to a new twist for afternoon snack time when you can see the steam dissipating from your children's creative play engine. Instead of tossing out a few apples to the crowd in front of the TV, a tiny bit of effort will pay off in a big way with an outdoor tea party. Find something to serve as a tablecloth, it could be an old tablecloth (I wouldn't use your great-grandmother's from the old country), a pretty towel or a spare sheet. Set an outdoor children's table, picnic table or small patio side table with some dishes you don't mind letting go out into the wild outdoors. Pop a little popcorn. Fill up the tea cups with some water and add a lemon wedge to the rim to fancy things up beyond the ordinary. Find a few other fun goodies to toss onto the table. The more miniature the snacks are the more intriguing they will seem. Have any small muffins? Fish shaped crackers? If you are the super, proactive, organized type and can plan ahead, freeze some ice cubes with edible flowers in them. How special is that? Have your children dress up for their tea party and let the afternoon tea time begin. It's not uncommon that in grown-up tea parties around the world participants play a game while enjoying their spot of tea. Help your children begin a fun little game of Eye-Spy using all the plants and animals surrounding them. They'll enjoy themselves while eating their snack, daring each other to bite the lemon and watching the ice cubes melt away revealing the edible flowers.

Let's Go to the Zoo

Materials: stuffed animals, snack

Got any stuffed animals that haven't seen the light of day in about a decade? If the answer was no, have a look under your child's bed. My guess is somewhere you may be able to find some old, stuffed friends that haven't been played with in quite some time. Well, let's subscribe to the theory what's old is new again. On a day of play when your child needs a creative boost, have your child take on the roles of both the zoo keeper and visitor with some old, familiar friends. Task one will be to haul those lost critters out of the toy box, out from under beds or wherever they may have been waiting and bring them outside. Have your child decide where each animal would be happiest in the zoo. A good task for an older child would be to try to match each animal to an area of the yard that might best represent that creature's habitat. Birds and monkeys may get assigned to some low hanging tree branches. Bears and anteaters (yes, they make those stuffed animals too) foraging at the bottoms of the trees. Deer might be found in the grass or meadow as the case may be. After each animal has been thoughtfully placed the zoo is ready for visitors. Now your child gets to walk around the zoo admiring his own work. If you have more than one child playing you might suggest from the start that the children take turns playing the role of zoo keeper. The zoo keeper can describe all sorts of interesting information about the animals to the zoo visitors. He may like to stop at the concession stand to pick up a little trail mix in a bag while enjoying the zoo. Some happy news is that these animals **CAN** be fed and it just so happens that their favorite food is whatever snack you packed in the bag!

Magic Carpet Ride

Materials: old (clean) rug, towel or "fancy" sheet, snack bag of glitter or sugar

Think you can scrounge up an old rug you've saved from before renovating the dining room? Do you have an ornate carpet with tassels on the ends rolled up in storage somewhere? That might be asking too much. Even if you can find a "fancy" sheet, blanket or towel you just found an afternoon of outdoor fun for your children. Bring your children outside with the "magic carpet" all rolled up. Tell them that you had forgotten all about this magic carpet stowed away in your house. When commanded where to go, this carpet will take children anywhere around the world AND get them back home by the dinner hour. Give each child his or her own bag of magic dust, a snack baggie of glitter or sugar in a pinch. This magic dust is what gives the magic carpet the lift it needs to fly around the world. Warn them to hold on tightly, the ride can be a little bumpy at times. Ask them where their first destination of choice will be. Like most books, movies or creative play ideas, you'll improve the storyline by supplying a plot or problem for your children to play with and solve. In a low, quiet voice warn your children that the sky is full of other magic carpet riders who are looking to take away some of your children's magic dust rendering the magic carpet useless. If the magic dust is taken from them, the rug will lose its ability to fly and your children will have to work together to find the magic dust thief, take back the dust and wisk themselves back home. The culprits looking to take the dust from your world travelers might be large crows flying in the trees above your yard or perhaps cars traveling on the street in front of your house. With that, unroll the magic carpet and send your explorers off for the afternoon. If upon unrolling the magic carpet you find that you and your children are suddenly lost in a dust storm, you may want to exchange this magic carpet for one in more presentable condition. Otherwise, tell them to enjoy the ride.

Hot Lava Hop

Materials: set of small plastic animals or other small items, two bowls, rocks or paper plates

For this play activity the grass in the yard will need to be transformed into hot lava …(thank goodness for childhood imagination, huh?). Strategically place a few rocks if you have them or paper plates throughout the yard creating a safe, hopping trail with a challenge level that is appropriate for your child. You might increase the level of difficulty for older children by adding a few obstacles along with way. Perhaps the more complicated, safe path goes through the swing set, over a stick and around a tree. At the start of the safe trail, place a container with the set of little, plastic animals or toys. Tailor this to the interest of your child with a box of favorite little objects. You might use 15 of his favorite match box cars, all your child's Strawberry Shortcakes, or a set of Legos. Find something that your child would be motivated to save. Now for the plot. Who is coming to try and take the treasured items or animals away? If it's the matchbox cars maybe the hot lava level is slowing rising and the cars must be saved before they're melted into a puddle of metal. If it's Strawberry Shortcake dolls maybe Purple Pie Man is coming to take away all the fruit from the dolls. If it's a container full of Legos maybe robotron is trying to smash them all into smithereens. You get the idea. Motivate your child to want to save the little collection of treasured items before it's too late. One by one each item must be carried to the "safety bucket" which is the container that you placed at the end of the safe trail near the last rock or paper plate. Your child must, clutching one treasured item at a time, navigate his way on the rocks to the other side of the hot lava never letting his foot touch the lava. Once the collection is again brought together in the safety bucket don't be surprised if your child's imagination takes over from here with a new story line involving the treasured items he saved and the dangerous, hot lava.

Long, Lost Adventure

Materials: backpack, messenger bag, or Grandpa's old briefcase, interesting items from the house

This activity capitalizes on the novelty of something new that is filled with surprises to be used in an enterprising way. Try to find your old, college backpack or any type of satchel you may have inadvertently saved for some reason yet unknown to mankind. You'll need to find one backpack type of bag per adventurer. Just don't go looking so deep in the basement that you can't find your way back out. Fill each backpack with items that could be used to fire up the imagination. Grab things like an old map, a magnifying glass, some yarn, an old sheet, some clothes pins, and don't forget a little, healthy snack for the adventurers. Once the supplies have been gathered your children and their imagination will take over and do the rest. Tell your children they're about to embark on an important exploration/discovery adventure. All the supplies they will need can be found in the backpack they'll be carrying along. Like all good storylines you might need to be ready to provide your adventurer with a plot or a problem. Perhaps bad weather is setting in and they'll need a shelter quickly constructed or maybe they've gotten lost and therefore must use the map to make their way back to base camp. Send them out the door with a kiss and a wave. Go well young travelers! It'll be fun to peek out the window and watch your children creatively playing together and discovering what emergency supplies can be found in their packs. Even better, watch how your young adventurers will put these items to good use in ways you may never have thought of. You may need to send along a little trail mix in case the supply of grubs and berries in their part of the world has been getting a little low.

BACKYARD
SCIENCE
EXPERIENCES

Ethogram

Materials: paper, pencil, hard surface to write on

What little outdoor creature do you have in your backyard that's moving all the time? No, your two year old doesn't count! You may not have even been aware but your yard is a metropolis of little animals scurrying about all day, or night. Tell your child she will conduct an animal study today using an ethogram. Never be afraid to use technical terms when talking with your children. They will learn more and develop more pointed questions when they are not spoken down to. For the ethogram choose an animal that you can guarantee will be putting on a pretty good show today. You want to choose an animal for observation that will be doing a variety of activities like eating, pausing, running, jumping, climbing, flying, walking, sleeping, attacking, chasing, carrying a nut, burying food, etc. Good animals to choose would be squirrels, ducks, geese, chipmunks or other little critters that stick around for a sufficient length of time to ensure your child can get some quality study time in. Along the left side of a sheet of paper write or sketch the activities/actions you could expect this particular animal to be seen doing. Many children love being given the responsibility of an important job. Explain to your child that she will be recording the actions she observes of this particular animal on her ethogram. Find a comfortable spot for her to observe the animal and have her start recording. One tally mark by each action she sees. The amount of time for observation will depend on the age and attention span of your child. You know her best. Make sure not to set the time so long that the project loses its appeal. I must say, it's a pretty impressive sight for passersby to see a three-year-old child sitting in the yard, peering through binoculars and scratching observations on her clipboard. That is, of course, until they ask what she's up to and she delightedly shares her findings that the ducks have pooped 17 times in the last 15 minutes. No matter the results, discuss her findings afterward. What can the two of you conclude about this animal? Now she can run outside and play imitating all the actions she just observed, well, most of them that is.

Fix It Shop

Materials: toy tools (ideally), or old mismatched tools

One of my favorite memories from my own childhood is laying on my stomach on the driveway "helping" my dad as he lay on his back under the car fixing something. Funny. Now that I think of it, that probably doesn't make his top ten list of favorites from back in the day. I do think he'll freely admit, however, there's just something intriguing about discovering the way things work. Looking under the car reveals, to me, nothing more than a confusing maze of pipes and tubes that apparently work together to make the car run. I must not have been attending well to our conversations under the car in those days. While it's not recommended to let your children lay under the car to independently discover the way things work I do know they love inspecting things like gears, tires, and chains working together to make something work. How about setting up a bike fix it shop in the garage? Turn every bike you feel comfortable with up-side-down so that they are resting on their seats and handle bars (probably best leave Dad's new titanium frame racer alone). That's all you'll need to do. Your child and her creativity will know how to begin conducting experiments with no further ado. It seems instinct takes over and children begin grabbing the pedals in front of them and start spinning the wheels. They'll love this new perspective on their bike. Scientific questions will bubble up in their busy minds. Why is only the back tire spinning? What does the chain grab on to? It's a physics lesson just waiting to happen. Of course, along with all this invaluable exploring and learning comes the inevitable tire banging, spoke adjusting and tube wrenching. This is why toy tools are ideal. Either way, flip those bikes up-side-down. The fix it shop is open for business. And don't you have an afternoon cup of coffee calling?

Walk with your Senses

Materials: paper, pencil, hard writing surface, trail mix

Observation and musement is an important part of childhood discovering and learning. As seasons change, observant children will see new colors in the yard. They may smell new smells, hear a new variety of birds in the yard and feel different textures and temperatures around them. Just sending your child outside and telling her to see what's new out there is often a little broad to really engage the young child. Help your child narrow her observation a bit and suddenly she will begin to see, hear, smell, taste and feel so much more. On a blank sheet of paper create two columns. The left column must be narrow with the majority of the paper being the right column. Now divide the paper into five horizontal sections using four lines. If I made myself clear you should have 10 quadrants. Five small ones on the left and five large ones on the right. Now draw a nose in the top spot of the left column. Under the nose draw an eye, under the eye draw an ear, under the ear draw a mouth, under the mouth draw a hand. You'll need one for each child involved (just when you thought you were through). Now your child has a tool to help narrow her search and observations, which will in fact, broaden her discoveries. Explain to your child that she should go outside and soak in her surroundings. She will draw what things she smells, draw what she is hearing, draw things she likes touching, draw what new things she saw that surprised her, finally she can draw her two favorite treats from the trail mix, rather that than gnawing on some oak tree bark to satisfy the senses. Your little biologist will head into the great outdoors and begin to experience her world and its changes with all her senses. She'll record her findings to share with you later. Have a meaningful discussion with her about what she found in the yard and how it made her feel. What surprised her? What surprised you? What was her favorite sense she used?

Big Bubbles

Materials: Joy Ultra or Dawn Ultra dish detergent, glycerin or Karo Syrup, water, utensils, 2 liter bottles cut in half

Step one: go outside. Step two: stay outside. Playing and exploring with large bubbles is fun and messy. Before your bubble blowers come inside be prepared to hose them off.

To create bubbles that hold together well follow this recipe:

Dawn Ultra or Joy Ultra - 1 part
Distilled Water - 15 parts
Glycerin or White Karo Syrup - 1/4 part*

Place all ingredients in a wide, flat container. Gently stir without creating foam. Now back away. Your children will take over with slotted spoons, a whisk, cheese grater, even a hanger pulled into the shape of a diamond. Anything they can find that has holes in it is worth experimenting with. You'll watch as your children's enthusiasm and creativity turns them into scientists conducting endless experiments with the bubbles and bubble wands. Our daughter found that the top half of a 2 liter bottle makes fantastic bubbles. They'll watch their friends or siblings' efforts to evaluate what works and what doesn't. This type of play is invaluable in the social and academic lessons it offers. On a side note, someone is bound to get a mouth full of soapy bubbles at some point. Guess they earned themselves a "free pass" for future use the next time they say something naughty. You may want to keep a glass of water handy for cleaning the soap away when needed.

*variation: try this recipe again in the winter on a very cold day. Blow a large bubble high in the air and watch it freeze as it floats toward the ground. You'll either see them shatter or careful hands may be able to pick them up to hold for a while.

*www.bubbleblowers.com

Nature Collector

Materials: milk jug belt (see page 30 for milk jug belt instructions)

One of the privileges of childhood is the right to muse, investigate, observe and explore. Most children will never again have this amount of free time to spend outdoors soaking up and experiencing the beauty of nature. Some of them will one day find themselves confined to a 10 foot by 10 foot office working 60 hours a week and perhaps be stuck underground in a subway on a 45 minute commute each day. Most of them will spend the vast majority of their time answering to someone else. When they come home from work there may not be much energy left but to turn on the TV and rest while another evening slips away. For your children today, time means nothing. The world is at their fingertips (or least the backyard for now). Strap on the milk jug belt and send your children to muse and explore in the yard. The task is for them to search and find the ten most interesting things that can be found in the yard. Send your children outside with the instructions to put anything they see as interesting into the belt. When the bucket is filled with wonderful things to ponder they spread them out on a flat surface and begin the rating process. Your children must choose the top ten items they find to be the most interesting and put them in the "keeper" pile. When the collection is complete this can be presented to you for the follow up discussion. Feel each item, smell it, shake it and listen. What does each item make your child feel or remind him of? What does each item remind you of or make you think of? Use this collection as a catalyst to spend some great time talking, pondering and musing together. It's important to your children that time be found to talk a bit together. Your daily tasks may prevent you from being able to discuss the findings immediately but try to make the time later that day to sit with your children and ponder over the curiosities he found in the yard.

Leaf Study

Materials: magnifying glass, paper, hard surface to write on, crayons

Innately, children love to learn. Leaves are all around us but has your child ever really been encouraged to look closely at the intricacies of a leaf? They really are marvels of nature. Your child doesn't have to be told the inner workings of the leaf to discover how amazing they are. Arm your child with a magnifying glass, a paper and a crayon. Ask him to find his favorite leaf in the yard. Now have him plop in the grass and begin really looking closely at this favorite leaf with the magnifying glass. Help get your child's leaf study started by drawing a larger outline of that leaf on the white paper. Ask your child to use his magnifying glass to look closely at the veins in the leaf. Have him map out the veins on his paper. The younger your child is the less accurate the veins will be and that's OK. The point is he is outside discovering a little about the world around him.

*How amazing is this?

- If you were to connect all the veins of an elm leaf, they would reach 700 feet!
- The veins help the water and photosynthesized food move in and out of the leaves in order to feed the tree.

*www.backyardnature.net –a website well worth a peek.

Water Play

Materials: large bucket of water or wading pool, variety of old, clean bottles, empty spice jars

Young children can learn so much by creative, sensory play with water. It is an important part of an enriched childhood. Without realizing it children learn about principles such as volume, water tension, gravity, cause and effect, before and after, among others just by playing and experimenting with water. Fill a wading pool or bucket with water at a comfortable temperature. Allow your child to experiment with some new "toys" such as a 2 liter plastic bottle with holes poked in the sides, a squeeze bottle, a plastic jar with holes poked in the lid to make a sprinkler, an eye dropper, a baster and any other water containers you can find in the house that could be used in an interesting way. Check your spice rack. If you have just a few granules of nutmeg, toss it in with your allspice and give your child a hand held water sprinkler. You'll see your child trying all sorts of experiments with water.

*Use special caution when your young children are playing with water. While the purpose of this book is to encourage your child to play independently, exception may need to be when using water with creative play. A comfortable rule of thumb for water play with young toddlers is to always stay an arm's length away from the child. A second aspect of safety is being sure the tools for water play and the water itself is clean. Children's hands are in the water conducting experiments and are likely to go to their mouths at anytime. Be sure to keep bacterial problems at bay by using clean tools and water for play. Children should also understand that the water is for play only. Water for drinking is found inside the house. Bearing all that safety mumbo jumbo in mind, let your child experience sensory play with water.

Taking Flight

Materials: several pages of paper a variety of different weights

Does your child enjoy designing and experimenting with different things? Is he or she nimble enough to fold a paper airplane? It doesn't have to be complex to undertake this experiment. The aircraft simply has to be able to stay afloat in the air for a short time. Teach the very young ones a single, classic paper airplane fold. Have the older child try several different types and perhaps even research it a bit on the computer. www.bestpaperairplanes.com is a great resource to begin with. Now equipped with several ideas of how to fold an airplane send your child outside to begin experimenting. Which fold design works the best? What type of paper flies the farthest? Later ask your child why he or she suspects that paper and fold design may have worked the best?

A word about closing doors on your child's development

Got a hunch your little one is not the "artsy" type? Maybe you think your child wouldn't be interested in paper airplanes. Let me make the case for why you, the parent, should never shut the door of opportunity on your child. I've been around children long enough to know that they are full of hidden talents and natural abilities. The only way you might help a child discover a new interest or ability is by exposing her to a wide variety of experiences. If you decide prematurely to keep your child away from certain experiences because you think she might not be interested or because you are not interested yourself, you've just narrowed the chances for your child to develop fully. Allow her to experience as much as you can possibly get your hands on. Adolescence and peer pressure will do plenty in the way of door closing at that stage. If you offer your children a childhood with a rich variety in experiences you'll allow them the opportunity to grow in abilities and self-confidence. How about these surprises, did you know Herschel Walker studied ballet? Julia Roberts plays a mean clarinet? Halle Barry is a skilled cartoonist? I'll let you catch the rest of the celebrity gossip at the magazine stand. My point is, let your child explore and experience every facet of play.

Seasonal Scavenger Hunt

Materials: milk jug belt (see page 30 for milk jug belt instructions), index card with pictured treasures

Watching the changing of the seasons can be an exciting prospect for young and old alike. To help your child learn to appreciate the way the yard demonstrates the changing seasons give your child an index card upon which you have drawn perhaps a dozen items that can be found outside and that reflect the changing season. The older children can probably handle more difficult items such as a four leaf clover, a basketball bug, a sassafras leaf, etc. You may even decide to write the words of the items to find next to the picture for them to get a little reading practice in at the same time. For a younger child, you may need to make an index card with fewer and simpler items to search for. Instead of a four leaf clover, include five blades of grass (try to get your young child counting as often as possible), four pine cones, three pieces of bark, two twigs, and a partridge in a pear tree… sorry…couldn't resist. If your young child is working on pre-reading skills you might include the first letter sound of each item's name he is searching for. As often as naturally possible it is beneficial to work in teachable moments that help enrich your young learner's experiences and develop his skills. When a child has found all the items on the list he can display them for review. Don't forget to praise your child for his hard work. Ask him a few good questions about the hunt and treasures that were found. Did he ever feel frustrated while searching? Why didn't he just give up? What was the easiest item to find? Which one was the most difficult? This is a good way for children to practice recalling and verbalizing an event that they have just experienced.

Sand Prints

Materials: sand box or box of moist sand, milk jug belt (see page 30 for milk jug belt instructions)

Has your child ever tried turning the sand box into an art palette? Encourage your young child to look at the possibilities in all objects by using them in new, innovative ways. She can have fun making all sorts of prints and patterns with flat, clean, moist sand. Help your child get set up for this activity by clearing out the sandbox of all the typical sandbox toys. If the sand is very dry you may need to spray a little water with the garden hose on the sand, stir it up and spray again. Moist sand holds its shape much better than dry sand. Your artist will be more successful and able to enjoy her prints for much longer in wet sand. When the sand is moist, smooth out the surface as flat as possible. Pack the sand down a bit and your child now has a beautiful new medium for her artwork. Encourage your artist to do some experimenting with all sorts of goodies that can be found in the yard. Strap on the milk jug belt and have her search around the yard for items she thinks could be pushed gently into the sand to make an interesting print or pattern. Perhaps she can find things to roll in the sand for a unique pattern. Some great examples are to try leaves of any sort, sturdy flowers, rocks or a pine needle cluster for printing. She might try rolling pine cones or thistles (carefully). With the milk jug belt full go back to the sand box and let the expression and experimenting begin. If it's warm enough outside, she may even decide to add a few footprints and handprints to her artwork. Encourage her to use creative, innovative ideas.

Shape Scavenger Hunt

Materials: shapes cut from construction paper, milk jug belt (see page 30 for milk jug belt instructions)

If your child is working on learning the names of shapes this project can be a great reinforcement of those skills. Cut a variety of shapes from some sturdy paper. The number and the variety is dependant on the age and ability of your child. If your child is in the early stages of learning the basics it will be challenging enough to offer a circle, square, triangle and rectangle. If this is all old hat for your child you can up the ante by going a little deeper into your shape knowledge base and giving him an octagon, a zig zag, an oval, trapezoid and a rhombus. If this starts sounding like alien speak just get creative with the scissors. The challenge for your child will be to take the stack of cards, or cut out shapes, strap on the milk jug belt and look for things in the yard that closely match each shape card they've been given. You may need to explain to a very literal child that finding a perfect shape in nature is very unusual but he can probably find an object that closely matches the shape card he's been given. Once a shape has been identified, gather up that item and stow it away in the milk jug belt with the card. One down, six to go. When the cards and natural items have all been tossed into the jug, your child should take out all of the collected items and match them back up with the shape card to display his findings. Take a look at how he did. Comment on what surprises you. Ask him which one was the most difficult to find. Which one was the easiest? Reward him for his efforts with a big circle (that's a hug by the way).

Dirt Digger

Materials: magnifying glass, bucket, shovel

Do you have access to a wild area of earth that has not been weed eated and fertilized? Got an area of the yard where you toss your watermelon rinds and peaches that turned fuzzy? If it's not too full of slimy leftovers grab a shovel and dig up some lively dirt for your child to explore in. I say lively because it's likely to be crawling with little goodies waiting to be discovered by an observant child. Before this activity your child may think that a bucket of dirt is simply that, a bucket of dirt. That theory couldn't be more wrong. Rather than explaining this to your child let him discover all that is to be found in a bucket of dirt. Let your child come with you to see where the dirt is being dug out from. Scoop out a good load of dirt and dump it into a bucket. Have your child hold the bucket so he can experience the weight of the dirt himself. Now your child can lug that bucket to an open area where the dirt can get dumped into a mountain of fun. Your child can use a magnifying glass to examine closely what's to be found in a bucket of dirt. He'll likely find little plants with small root systems, earthworms, possibly some litter, old rotting leaves, twigs turning to dirt, and all sorts of other surprises. After your child has been given sufficient time to examine every aspect of the items discovered, talk together about what makes healthy dirt and what harms the dirt. If he tosses his granola bar wrapper on the ground how does that affect the soil and organisms found there? You can point out that the old leaves and twigs help make fertile soil for that growing plant. The roots will "eat" the nutrients left by those leaves and twigs while the earthworm aerates the soil making it fertile. If your child is interested you might encourage him to sort the goodies found into categories like which things are alive and which are inanimate. He may be surprised that many things found in a bucket of dirt are alive or were at one time. Not a bad bunch of learning for a bucket full of dirt.

Bubble Tower

Materials: bubble solution (see bubble solution recipe on page 87), wading pool, hula hoop

Bubbles are magical little marvels to watch floating through the air. How would your child like to be in the center of one of those bubbles without having to shrink down to the size of his big toe? Fill a wading pool with about 2 inches of bubble solution. Your child must stand in the center of the pool and place a hula hoop on the bottom of the pool surrounding him. Caution: the Karo Syrup makes the floor of the pool hazardously slippery. You may need to use a pair of socks or rubber boots on your child to ward off the concussion risk. Your child can slowly raise the hula hoop and find himself surrounded by a wall of bubbles. It may take some patience to get it just right but if the ingredients were measured correctly he'll become the boy in the bubble, until the inevitable finger poke that is.

Make Raisins

Materials: cookie sheet or other flat dish, bunch of grapes, bowl of water, sunshine

Many children love eating sweet tasting raisins. Parents are happy because there's a decent amount of minerals found in raisins. If your child happens to be one that doesn't like the taste or texture of raisins, odds are she will at least enjoy making raisins the same way Native Americans used to make the tasty treat. Your child might be interested to know that most of the world's raisins come from California. The majority of raisins there are left to sun-dry on the vine which is a process that takes a couple of weeks. Then they are harvested, cleaned and shipped out to us, the consumers. Your child can get a first hand experience in the raisin making process. Have her sit outside with a bunch of grapes and a bowl of water. Each grape will need to be washed in the water to be free from pesticides, dirt and other yuckies. After each grape has been cleaned it can be placed on the cookie sheet. When the sheet is filled cover the grapes with a breathable cloth and weigh the cloth down with rocks so no curious animals can sneak a peek. Let the raisins 'cook' in the sun for several days. Have your child take a peek from time to time and perhaps even a taste test. Your child will know when the time is right to stop the 'cooking' and enjoy the treat. Yummmm.

*one other raisin tidbit: did you know that in ancient Roman days a slave could be traded for 2 jars of raisins?

Perspective

Materials: two pieces of paper, pencil, hard surface to write on

Looking at the same object from a different perspective can be a challenge. Have you ever shown your child her bedroom, which she is so familiar with, from the outside of the house? Same room, but as she's peering through the window it takes on a whole new feel. Changing your child's perspective can make something very familiar feel a little unfamiliar just by looking from a new angle. Ask your child to sit in front of your house and draw everything she sees. She'll likely be very familiar with what the front of her house looks like. Instruct her to include the details she sees on the house as well as in the yard. Can she see anything in the windows to include in the drawing? Now set her up for the challenge. Imagine what the house and yard must look like from a bird's perspective or bird's eye view. Same house, but it will take on a whole different feel. Starting with a new sheet of paper, ask your child to walk around the house or sit wherever needed and draw the house from a bird's eye view. Suddenly, her house is going to feel a bit unfamiliar. Again, instruct her to include any details she can see on the house as well as the yard that a bird would see from above. Talk together about how the drawings are the same and how they are different. Ask your child which one was more difficult to draw? What made it more challenging? Be sure to display her work somewhere prominently for a few days.

*variation: if this activity is at a level that you know is too difficult and frustrating for your young child, start with something simpler such as a flower or interesting bush in the yard. The process will be the same. Your child will draw the object from the front in great detail. Next she should draw the same object from the bird's eye view. You can simplify the task by choosing an object to draw that can be viewed and sketched from the top as well as from the front. The follow up discussion can be the same.

What Floats?

Materials: wading pool, items from the yard

There are so many physical properties a child can discover and experiment with in water play it isn't even funny. Just exploring with water teaches a child that water is actually rather sticky. It likes to clump together. This is called water tension. Water would rather stick together in the form of a drop as opposed to spread out super flat over a wide area. The temperature of water changes relatively slowly. Your child will notice, over time, that cool air temperatures will slowly cool the water he is playing in. Hot air temperatures will slowly warm the water he is playing in. We haven't even begun to list all the physical, cognitive and developmental benefits of water play. Help your child to experience these fascinating water principles by simply setting up creative play in a vat of water. Fill a wading pool, or some such tub, with water and ask your child to find a variety of things from the yard to experiment with what floats and what sinks. Test all these things out in the water and then go back for more to try. The next objective for your child will be to try to take the things that sank and find a way to make them float across the water from one side to the other. Hopefully he'll try to float the sinking objects, like small stones, on large enough leaves that will act as a boat. The surface tension of the water will allow the leaves to stay afloat. If the leaves are large enough they will carry the stones across the pool. After play has gone on for a good while point out to your child the drops of water that he might see collecting on the leaf. Use the term "water tension" to explain that water droplets like to stick together rather than spread out. Where else do we see water droplets sticking together to form bigger drops? (rain drops) Did your child notice a slow change in the temperature of the water while he was playing? Talk together for a few minutes while cleaning up about the water principles that your child just experienced.

Size Scavenger Hunt

Materials: construction paper cut into squares and rectangles of various sizes (1 set per hunter), milk jug belt (see page for 30 for milk jug belt instructions)

Your child's outdoor world is filled with items of all different sizes, some already discovered, some yet undiscovered. Each new season brings about its own specific, new treasures. The basketball bug crawling in the woodchips all summer is no where to be found in the early, winter days. The rhododendron leaves that are curled up tightly on cold, winter days are wide open and flat in the hot summer. This scavenger hunt might be fun for your child to play once each season so that she might experience and compare what's new to be found as the seasons change. Hook the milk jug belt around your child's waist again so your hunter can gather goodies and have two free hands to continue her investigating. The object of the game is to match the size of the construction paper card to an object outdoors that best fits that card's size. For example, a small square the size of a quarter might be best matched with an acorn or pebble. A large, wide rectangle may be filled best by an oak leaf. Please explain to your searcher that she will not find something to fill the card exactly (otherwise some literal children will never make it back to the house). This card is only meant to serve as a guide for size. The hunter must find something that just about fills the card. When she has found the item, toss the card and the treasure into the milk jug belt and go on to the next card. When each of the cards has been matched with an object and tossed into the jug, your child can find an open flat area to display all her finds. She should lay the cards out on the walkway, deck or other flat area and cover each card with its matching item to be overlooked by you. Be sure to praise your child for her hard work and determination. Talk about which size card was the hardest to find, which one was the favorite, how might the results be different in a new season? Does the biggest shape always match with the heaviest object?

Beat That Bubble

Materials: bubble solution(see bubble solution recipe on page 87), bubble wand, tape measure

Just simply blowing bubbles can be old hat if you're a "big kid" i.e. 5¾ years old. You can easily up the ante to help children stay intrigued by the magic of blowing bubbles. Charge them with blowing the biggest bubble on record. They have to go outside and find a clear area of cement like a patio, driveway or walkway to play in. Your child can warm up by gently blowing bubbles. Once she has her technique perfected it's time to go on record. She should blow a bubble as large as possible. Watch that bubble float. As it's working its was through the air your child can grab her tape measure and get ready for action. Wherever the bubble lands it will pop and leave a nice, wet spot on the cement. Explain to your child that measuring from one edge of the wet circle to the other edge gives the diameter of the bubble. She can try different blowing techniques and perhaps a variety of bubble wands. The challenge to create the biggest bubble on record will keep her working. A tip from our house that makes life easier: I keep our bubble solution in a big bucket with a lid in the garage. When we come home from grocery shopping and I need to organize the groceries in the house, I first take out the bubble bucket. They have their own fun and I get the work done. You might be surprised how often you will use the bubble bucket for a quick ten minutes of play for your children while you get something accomplished.

By the way, *"On October 9, 2005, John Erck of XTREME Bubbles blew the Guinness World Record largest free-floating soap bubble, 105.4 cubic feet (2.98 cubic meters) in size. If the bubble were filled with water, it would hold 788 gallons and weigh 3.2 tons. To give you another idea of its size, 13,627 baseballs would fit inside of it." Just in case you wanted to set the bar high.

*www. bubbleblowers.com

Leaf Match Up

Materials: brown paper lunch bag, ten different leaves from the yard, milk jug belt (see page 30 for milk jug belt instructions)

Ovate, elliptic, round, lobed, rhomboid, spathulate, oblanceolate. Have you heard? Disney's changing the names of the seven dwarfs. Did I get you there for a moment? These are actually just a tiny fraction of the names given to the variety of shapes leaves come in. Has your child ever taken the time to really look at the wide range of leaf shapes that can be found in his own yard? Five minutes of your time is all that is needed to get your child into an activity that will have him observing, sorting, categorizing and matching leaves from his own yard. Take a brown, paper lunch bag and make a quick cruise throughout the yard. Your goal is ten. Ten different leaves from throughout your yard need to go into the bag. Leaves of trees obviously count but so do the leaves of bushes, vines, flowers and grasses, like clover leaves. Pine needles are leaves as well. Once you've found a good sampling of leaves, bring the bag back to your child and challenge him to find the match for each of the leaves in the bag. Strap on the milk jug belt for your child to put the matched leaves in so they all don't become one big, confusing mix of greens. You will now see your child thinking critically while inspecting each plant like a botanist. Upon approaching each tree, bush or flower your child will have to ask himself what shape are these leaves? Are the edges smooth or jagged? Is there a pattern to the shape of the leaves on the tree that matches the one in my hand? Does this leaf look familiar? If the leaf is a winner, in the milk jug belt it goes. When your child finds that his bag is empty and the jug is full he knows that all the leaves have been matched. Next task will be to lay them out, matched with their pair, for display. Talk with your child about his findings and see how many leaf types the two of you can name.

Nature Exhibit

Materials: yard full of goodies, prominent area for display, milk jug belt (see page 30 for milk jug belt instructions)

If you've ever lived in the same house as a child who just developed oral language skills you know that aged child likes to share her ideas… A LOT! It's not uncommon to see a two-year-old trailing along behind her mother or father jabbering away intently about everything she is thinking about, observing, wondering about, pontificating on. What they lack in their abilities to share in toys children at this stage more than compensate for in ability to share in knowledge. Who knew one human being could gain so much wisdom in just two short years? Use your young child's desire to share her thoughts and opinions with you in outdoor play. Strap on the milk jug belt and tell her to choose some favorite things she can find outside and store them in her milk jug belt. When the belt is full she can display her treasures so that all might stop and marvel at her discoveries. You might clear off a section of some shelves for the day or perhaps the coffee table could use a facelift with a smattering of outdoor items. Tell your child to display her items and then discuss the discoveries with her. Where did she find a particular stone? What color is it? Which item is her favorite? Which item is yours? Have fun marveling together over her nature exhibit.

Bubbletown

Materials: bubble solution (bubble solution recipe on page 87), straw, rimmed cookie sheet, little plastic figurine

The materials listed above might look like a recipe for disaster. Bubble solution and a straw? Seriously?!? If your child is old enough to follow the instructions to blow through a straw and NOT use it for sucking she can try this bubble fun. If you think for a moment your child might suck in the solution instead of blow out from sheer habit or your child is too young to comprehend these instructions you better return to this activity at a later date. Pour some bubble solution on a wide, flat dish like a rimmed cookie sheet or large casserole and give your child a straw. Set him up outside where making a bubble mess can disappear into the grass instead of scrubbing off the kitchen floor. Have him start blowing bubbles in the bottom of the pan using the straw, you know, using the method he's always told not to do in his milk cup (milk bubbles are some of the best, aren't they?). Once a good amount of bubbles has been worked up tell your child to put his straw inside one of the bubbles and start blowing. He'll watch this bubble overgrow into a huge, bubble giant. Now let the fun experimenting begin. He'll be growing and popping all kinds of bubbles. Put a little plastic character in the bubble universe and your child will be able to create a complete bubble town for this little someone. If your child wets his hands, which they probably already are from all the bubble popping, he'll stand a chance at picking up some of the bubbles without causing them to pop immediately. Word of warning; If you see your child getting a little too carried away in all the fun and beginning to turn blue in the face or he's starting to swoon, it may be time to take a little bubble blowing break.

FUN WITH
SIDEWALK
CHALK

The Perfect Picnic

Materials: sidewalk chalk

How about a spread of macaroni and cheese, gum balls, a plate of pickles, chocolate kisses, licorice, and a side of cotton candy? Think your child would finish her plate without hounding her in that meal? Draw a large rectangle on the sidewalk or driveway and tell her that she is in charge of feeding the two of you. Have her draw all her favorite foods that she would plan for the Best Dinner Ever. She can set the table by drawing the plates, cups and utensils. Next, she can fill up the center of the table by drawing a spread like no one has ever seen before. Any food she has ever had that could be categorized as a "favorite" gets a spot on this table. She can fill the serving platters as well as your plate and her plate. When the table is full and the food is prepared have a seat at your spot and pig out!

*sidewalk chalk fun fact: If your children have ever gotten their hands on a Twinkie, odds are they have asked, if not begged, for another. How about this for hitting the jack pot? When I was in third grade a girl in my class used to ask me if I would trade my bag of peanuts and raisins for her Twinkies! Cha-ching! As you might imagine I was none too happy about not seeing her name on my class list the next year. My Twinkie days were over, but I digress. My point in mentioning this is not to brag about my incredible elementary score. Rather, did you know that Twinkies and chalk are both made using the same ingredient? They each contain gypsum, otherwise known as calcium sulfate. It's also in drywall and tofu. How about trying that one next time for your argument against Twinkies. Although you may find a Mr. Smarty Pants then trying to gnaw on a chalk stick hoping for a hint of that tempting snack cake.

Home Sweet Home

Materials: sidewalk chalk

Children love to play house. Even in a house made of chalk. After talking to scads of parents and watching children play it seems the most creative fun is had when the frame of the house is drawn for your child from the front view, as though the front wall of the house has been taken down. What you draw for your child is a huge version of what a dollhouse looks like. You might draw two large empty rooms on the main floor, three small rooms on the second floor and one large room on the third floor. It is now up to your child to put in stairs, an elevator and perhaps a waterslide to traverse from floor to floor. Encourage them to add furnishings, flooring and doo dads on the walls. Don't forget your child will need to include windows and landscaping in the yard. The more creative your suggestions are in the beginning, the more likely your child's creativity will be tapped. Once the construction in the kitchen has been completed you might decide to offer your architect a few grapes or an apple. Knock on the door and pop over to enjoy a little snack with your child in his kitchen.

*a tip about sidewalk chalk: if you let a couple of sidewalk chalk sticks rest in a jar with about an inch of water on the bottom your child's artwork will become more vivid and bright. Chalk lays on more thickly when it is wet which is why your child's art work will be dramatically brighter and more colorful. The flip side is that you'll have to add sidewalk chalk to the grocery list more frequently.

Lost your Marbles

Materials: marbles, sidewalk chalk, string

It's easy to picture your grandfather as a child quaintly playing marbles in the dirt packed streets with the neighborhood kids. Are you picturing it in black and white? Me too, with a hint of sepia. Marbles seem like a game of the past. We've got DVD players providing excitement for our kids to look at and video games keeping our kids' thumbs active. Pause (brakes' screeching sound effect in the background). Instead of staring mutely at a TV screen, get your child out there with other kids interacting, strategizing, soaking up Vitamin D and entertaining himself. These are all extremely important life skills for successful people of today that cannot be absorbed from an electronic screen. So, draw a circle in the cement two or three feet wide. Next, take a set of marbles and select one "Shooter" for each player. The shooter should be a little larger than the other marbles so it has the power to knock the little guys around a bit. The small marbles go inside the circle and the players kneel outside the circle. Taking turns, each player sets her shooter marble on the cement and flicks it using her thumb toward the smaller marbles inside the circle (See? Thumbs can still get their workout too). If she knocks a marble out of the circle she takes that marble as well as the shooter. She shoots again if a marble got knocked out. If nothing happened, she gathers up her shooter and waits her turn. Play ends when all the marbles have been knocked out of the ring. Return the small marbles to their original owner unless you're playing for "keepsies". In that case you get to keep what you've captured.

*variation: we've found that some chubby little fingers just aren't nimble enough to flick that shooter in the direction it's meant to go and that can bring on the waterworks. If you're trying for marbles with very young children use some string to create a circle about six feet wide in the grass. Fill that circle with some bouncy, playground type balls. Play is the same as regular marbles except each player throws or rolls a ball at the target ball instead of a marble. Again, winner gets to keep the balls she knocked out.

Train Station

Materials: sidewalk chalk, yard stick or other long, flat piece of wood, duct tape

Got a little one who can't get enough 'train' in the day? There's something about the rumble of the engine, the magnificent power of the train and the speed at which it zooms by that leaves some children in quiet awe, which at times is no easy task. Use that insatiable interest for some great outdoor, creative play. Instead of playing with toy trains on the living room floor again have your child turn into a train for the day. Draw train tracks down the driveway, up the sidewalk and over to the walkway. I did find drawing all these lines on my hands and knees a little tiresome. After shuffling forward on my knees drawing chalk lines for railroad tracks for about 12 feet I was looking for a better method. So were my knees. I thought of jamming the chalk in the turkey baster minus the bulb but then realized I struggle with keeping turkey moist enough let alone adding chalk to the problem. I found that if you take a moment to tape the chalk to a yard stick with strong tape like duct tape, you'll find that laying the tracks becomes much easier and quicker. Your knees will thank you. Get creative and draw these train tracks across the lawn. Faded though it may be, chalk does draw lines on grass. Get that train chugging around trees and over rocks, past puddles and swooping by the swing set. Once the tracks have been set up your train is ready for take off. Creative play always gets an extra shot in the arm when an imaginary problem is introduced that must be resolved. Lay a few, large sticks over the tracks, find a stone to interrupt the pathway, do you have a cow in the house? (stuffed hopefully) Lay him on the tracks too. By creating problems for your child to solve you'll extend his playtime and help him create an imaginary storyline to develop. Experiencing simple problems and solutions are great prewriting skills for your young child to become familiar with. Now chug along inside and fire another couple engines up--the vacuum and the coffee pot.

Cloud Animals

Materials: white crayon, blue paper, hard writing surface or side walk chalk

Every now and again the weather conditions are just right so that the clouds floating by are big, white and fluffy. With a great imagination almost any of these beautiful clouds can be turned into an image. For the beginner, it's best to try this activity on a day that the sky is full of those shapely, fluffy clouds. Just for the record these clouds are called cumulus clouds, and they usually indicate a dry weather day which also happens to be perfect conditions for playing, observing and drawing outside. Help your child get started by setting her up in a great cloud viewing spot in the yard. Wherever she can be with the least sky obstruction is perfect. If she is going to draw on paper the images she sees in the sky she can choose any spot in the yard. However, if she's going to draw the images with sidewalk chalk she'll need to get comfortable near some concrete. Once you've helped get the observation station set up with a comfortable position for your child and drawing materials handy she is set to begin her task. Your child will enjoy laying back in the grass and watching clouds float on by. After several minutes of observation she'll likely begin to notice that many of the clouds are slowing changing shape as they move across the blue sky. Not every cloud will appear to take on the image of something. Be patient, watch and wait. Suddenly she might see an animal will come floating by. How exciting! Your child then should try to copy what she sees in the sky onto her paper or on the sidewalk. The more animals she sees the easier this task will become. If your child is struggling with seeing anything in the clouds, lay down next to her to spot a few examples that you can see. Draw one example together. This will help her better understand the task at hand. A creative eye can find a pretty strange menagerie of animals. Our children have spotted a snake with a duck's head floating by, a sheep with wings and many other fun, crazy combos. Let your child have fun and be inventive with what she finds. The sky is the limit…no pun intended.

Zany Hopscotch

Materials: sidewalk chalk

Who doesn't like the challenge of hopping along the squares and rectangles in the rousing game of hopscotch? Switch things up a bit and make it even more eventful and educational by taking hopscotch to a whole new level. If your child is learning to count or working on the ABC's this activity can be a fun way to review those skills. Begin by drawing the traditional square with a letter or number as a starting point. Rather than continuing on with the two connected squares on top, Zany Hopscotch will surprise and tickle your child at every turn. It becomes somewhat of an obstacle course. You'll need to get creative. Your child may have to jump over a branch to reach the triangle with the number 2 or letter B. The third spot may be next to a bucket of water in which your child has to dip his forehead in (on a hot day). Think outside of the box and try all sorts of zany ideas. Here's a few more to consider; twirl a spiral, walk through a hula hoop, circle around a sprinkler before reaching the next shape and number or letter, jump rope 10 jumps, juggle, shoot a basket, break dance to some tunes, look through some binoculars at a bird or unsuspecting neighbor, do a donkey kick, fling a yo-yo, beller out your favorite animal sound, sing a song, blow bubbles, run around a bush, do a handstand (this one may be best attempted in the grass), drink a whole glass of water, eat a carrot, decorate the shape you are on with some sidewalk chalk. Be sure to mix up the shapes using as many as you can think of and have your child call out the letter or number they have just reached. If you've reached the end of the numbers your child is familiar with this game is also a great way to review other skills your child is working on. How about calling out the shape her feet are on? Count and call out the number of dots inside the shape he just landed on. Be creative and have fun yourself. Why simply be square?

Field Trip

Materials: sidewalk chalk

Is there a special outing your child likes to go on? Does she have a favorite museum, a love for the library? How about taking a stroll through a historic downtown? Whatever her pleasure is you can recreate it! Meeting the responsibilities of life often stand in the way of being able to travel wherever our hearts might desire. If that were not the case I'd be lounging around the beach in Cancun right now. Help get your child's imagination geared up by sketching the outline of her favorite place to visit. If she likes the local museum begin together by using sidewalk chalk to draw the familiar entrance to the museum and let her memory and her imagination take over from there. Is it the library she fancies? You might start together by drawing the main points of the floor plan and let her take over filling in all of her favorite sections she visits. The choices are endless. Encourage your child to expand on what is at this location in reality. Now you're into some higher order thinking! What kinds of exhibits should this museum offer? Draw what they might look like. How could the library be even better than it already is? My children added two extra candy stores to their downtown. After your child has drawn and planned and worked and played take the time to ask her to explain her drawing to you. It's great practice for her brain to retell her experiences. It's also a great way for you to learn more about what makes your little person tick.

Strike a Pose

Materials: sidewalk chalk

Have you ever watched a child experimenting with his shadow? I think that must be where the phrase simple pleasures came from. Children are so intrigued by that dark playmate always by their side on a sunny day. Encourage your children to do more exploring with their shadow. This activity works best with two or more children involved. Start by helping your children find a good spot on the driveway to cast their shadow. One child will start as the poser and the other the sketcher. This type of play, by the way, helps instill the ability to work as a team. Each child must take on a different role to successfully complete the task. Whatever silly pose the first child comes up with, the sketcher will trace the outline of the shadow on the cement. Now the children switch roles. A new pose is then sketched on the cement. Encourage your children to get creative and silly. They might decide to connect their poses into one large mural. They can pose themselves into letters and try to spell a word, or they can simply be goofy and have fun looking back at the expressions of themselves. Don't forget about the possibility of using props to enhance their ideas.

Under the Sea

Materials: sidewalk chalk

If you've ever looked into the eyes of a child in an aquarium you know that the underwater world is a magical mystery to him. Every fish has a different face to see, the friendly sea turtle bobbles by, even the hypnotic shark demands a child's admiration. Recreate this magic using your child's imagination right in the driveway. Start by drawing large tanks, or rectangles around the perimeter of the driveway. Your child will decide who will reside in each tank. You might decide to draw a large square with an island inside for a dolphin show venue. Don't forget to include a few benches for your child to sit and watch the show when the dolphins are drawn and ready. Once the construction of the aquarium has been complete your child can begin filling each tank with all of the sea creatures he knows about. Don't interfere if he puts the Great White Shark in with the Giant Pacific Octopus and a lost Emperor Penguin. You and the penguin can just quietly be grateful he's not the curator of an aquarium quite yet. If your child needs a resource for more underwater creature ideas, tell him to check through all the reading books you may have available or have a peek on the computer at an aquarium's website.

*variation: if your child has no personal experience or you think he'd rather draw his animals in the wild you may simply draw the ocean floor and perhaps a sunken ship. He can then begin to draw the water teeming with delightful and daring creatures.

*sea animal fun fact: Whale sharks are pretty incredible animals to familiarize your child with. Grab a tape measure and some chalk. Draw a fish on the driveway that measures 46 feet in length. Put a great, big smiley face on that guy. That is how large an actual whale shark can be. Quite something to behold right there in front of your child. Whale sharks are covered in polka dots. Your child can add 46 feet worth of dots to the shark. That'll be a day of play in itself! By the way, they only eat plankton and tiny fish in case your child asks. That great big guy is more friend than foe.